BING CROSBY

BING CROSBY

A Pyramid Illustrated History of the Movies

by
BARBARA BAUER

General Editor: **TED SENNETT**

PUBLICATIONS
NEW YORK

To the three people who are for me
"what life is all about"—
Mr. and Mrs. Ervin Bauer and Robert F. Moss.

BING CROSBY
A Pyramid Illustrated History of the Movies

A PYRAMID BOOK

Pyramid edition published June 1977

Library of Congress Catalog Card Number: 77-5264

Printed in the United States of America

Pyramid Books are published by Pyramid Publications (Harcourt Brace Jovanovich, Inc.). Its trademarks, consisting of the word "Pyramid" and the portrayal of a pyramid, are registered in the United States Patent Office.

Pyramid Publications
(Harcourt Brace Jovanovich, Inc.)
757 Third Avenue, New York, N.Y. 10017

Layout and Design by ANTHONY BASILE

ACKNOWLEDGMENTS

My very special thanks to Joe Seechack, Mike Stephens, Mel Neuhaus, Elizabeth Murphy, and Wence Torres of New York's Channel 5 (WNEW), who turned over to me their wonderfully rich library of Bing Crosby films and who gave me a screening room, ran the projectors, shared their awe-inspiring fund of Crosbiana, and brought me coffee during my long but delightful days of movie viewing.

Thanks also to the staff of the fine film section of New York University's Bobst Library and to the staff of the Research Division of the Lincoln Center Library. The impressive files, fully-stocked shelves, and helpful associates of these two organizations make research a pleasant task.

I am also grateful to the employees of the Strand Bookstore who found for me books on Crosby that no other bookstore seemed to have and, especially, to the film buffs at Cinemabilia, who located special and unusual Crosby treasures and held them for me—despite the clamorings for relevant material of radio and television stations and journalists that preceded Mr. Crosby's Broadway appearance.

I would also like to thank Bernie Green for his efforts with Mr. Crosby on my behalf, not the least of which was that special seat at the Uris Theatre, and Dale Burg for keeping a watchful eye out for Crosby screenings and newspaper stories that I might have missed.

My greatest debt of thanks is to Ted Sennett, who has spoiled me for all editors to come.

And, finally, I would like to add my appreciation of the support and kindness of Barbara Jarocki and Robert Fudim, two very special people whom it is an honor to know.

Photographs: Jerry Vermilye, The Memory Shop, Gene Andrewski, and the companies that produced and distributed the films of Bing Crosby

CONTENTS

In *Here Comes the Groom*, Jane Wyman tells Bing Crosby that she's known men who were better looking, richer, and taller. In *The Emperor Waltz*, Joan Fontaine tells him that her first husband made her the envy of Vienna. He was dark and distinguished. "You're so different," she sighs.

Bing *is* different. Certainly there have been better voices, better actors, flashier public personalities. But there have been few success stories as remarkable. Past generations warmly remember Crosby's heyday. We of more recent generations, however, regard Bing Crosby as we do certain old "standards." We hear these songs played occasionally, recognize the melodies, and can sing snatches of the lyrics. They conjure up furtive moonlight kisses and dancing cheek-to-cheek. Other than that, we don't think about them. They've just always been around—and so, it seems, has Bing.

Gather a group of people under age forty in a room and see how many of Bing Crosby's films they can name. Ask them who—including both groups and solo performers—has sold the greatest number of records in history. Ask them to name the number one best-selling record of all time. Many would have to grope for the answers.

Bing did not just travel roads to far-off places with Bob Hope and

THE BING THING

"Some fellas got it and some fellas ain't got it. I got it."
Bing Crosby—*Road to Zanzibar*

Dorothy Lamour or keep the wayward boys of his parish off the streets by teaching them to sing. More Crosby movies rank among the all-time moneymakers than those of any other performer. He made over seventy films in a career that has spanned five decades. For two of those decades, he was one of the country's biggest box office stars—while, at the same time, hosting the most popular show on radio. With record sales of over 400,000,000, he is the most successful recording artist in the history of the industry. His rendition of "White Christmas" is the biggest-selling record ever produced. Second is his recording of "Silent Night."

Most of us have forgotten—or have never realized—how spectacular are the statistics of his career, how impressive the range of his talents, how just plain good he is. And yet, despite these formidable credentials, we have trouble pinpointing the cause of his gargantuan success, especially in his films. His ears are so flappy that the studio had to pin them back. He is short and was at times so stocky that he was forced to wear a girdle. And the Crosby toupée was well-known industry gossip before he decided to make it a running gag. Even with all of Paramount's improvements, he was never—outside of his regular features and very blue eyes—classic leading man material. Still, he usually got the girl, and when she told him she loved him, we believed her.

Why? Because Bing Crosby has a style all his own. A charming, casual, crooning style that disarms us. It always appears as if his singing or acting or clowning or crying are the most natural things in the world. Bing's thing is that he makes it all seem so easy.

Except for his Irish-Catholic heritage, Bing Crosby's background is almost archetypally Middle American. Descended from solid New England stock on his father's side and from Irish immigrants on his mother's, Harry Lillis Crosby was born in Tacoma, Washington, on May 2, 1901, the fourth of seven children, and raised in Spokane. His famous nickname, which he earned at age nine, came from "The Bingsville Bugle," a popular comic strip in which the principal character had big ears. His father was a bookkeeper in a brewery, and Bing's modest but comfortable upbringing seems to have been commonplace and uneventful. Sports and music were the two chief interests he carried through high school and on into college.

At Gonzaga University, Crosby majored in law and worked part-time for a Spokane law firm. He was, however, much more excited about singing and playing drums with a small combo called the Musicaladers. Though he'd never had a formal music lesson (he still hasn't), Bing yearned for a singing career. When the Musicaladers dissolved in 1925, he and fellow alumnus Al Rinker drove to Los Angeles in hopes of crashing show business. Al's sister, Mildred Bailey, a well-known vocalist of the period, created an entrée for the boys, and they moved quickly from a small

ALL ABOUT BING

local theater to the Fanchon and Marco vaudeville circuit and then on to a permanent job with Paul Whiteman's band. There Harry Barris joined them, and they became the Rhythm Boys.

Crosby's talent was obvious to everyone at this time, but so was his lackadaisical approach toward work and his weakness for a girl, a bottle, and a good time. His career had its ups and downs before a successful radio broadcast and a spectacular show at the Paramount Theater in New York (both in the fall of 1931) made him an unquestionable star.

Around this time, Everett Crosby had stepped in to manage his brother's rather bumpy career. He was able to negotiate contracts so unimaginably lavish that, according to brother Bob, "when the first paycheck came in, Bing's eyes bugged out at the size of it." Whether it was the money or Everett's businesslike approach or the success at the Paramount, Bing finally settled down.

As a relative unknown, Crosby had made six inconsequential shorts for Mack Sennett in the summer of 1931 (and had played some part in other films), but now, beginning with *The Big Broadcast* (1932), he embarked on a full-scale film career. A long series of bright-eyed musical comedies followed (e.g., *College Humor, She Loves Me Not, Rhythm on the Range*), establishing him as one of the biggest and most lucrative names on the Hollywood roster. Though co-workers called him a "fast study" and a dedicated artist, and praised his unusual talent for making even the toughest scenes look easy, they also noted his occasional relapses into irresponsibility and dissipation—which generally took the form of drinking sprees with his buddies. His fans didn't mind, however; by 1934 he was receiving 10,000 letters a week and had eighty-five fan clubs. From this year onward, he also hosted one of the country's most popular radio shows; it did not leave the air until 1956.

Some people have accused Bing of false modesty when he credits his success with sounding just like anyone who sings in the shower. Perhaps the modesty was not that false. He inserted a stipulation into his contract with Paramount that he was not to be starred alone. "I feel if a picture's good," he said, "everybody should share the credit for it. And if it's bad, we should all go down swinging together."

In his private life, Bing enjoyed a domestic stability that was quite uncommon in Hollywood. He and his wife, Dixie Lee, a 20th Century-Fox starlet whom he married in September 1930, remained devoted

to one another. In 1933, she bore him the first of four sons, Gary. Twins, Phillip and Dennis, followed in 1934, and the last boy, Lindsay, was born in 1937.

Bing's days as a reckless free-spender—there was a time when his expenses always ran ahead of his salary—ended with the beginning of his film career. Flanked by Everett and a shrewd Paramount lawyer named John O'Melveny, Bing began his long march to the fabled wealth that is now as much a part of his legend as his "boo-boo-boo." In partnership with Bob Hope, he purchased several small oil companies, which eventually paid off handsomely. Nevertheless, it's hard to believe O'Melveny's claim that today these are Crosby's principal sources of income, since he has, over the years, held large or controlling interests in Santa Anita Racetrack, the Del Mar Turf Club, the Pittsburgh Pirates, and a number of banks. A daring investment in frozen orange juice, an unproven product at the time, resulted in ownership of Minute Maid. Estimates of Bing's wealth range from $150 million (Hope) to $3.5 million (Crosby himself).

During World War II, Bing was closely identified with patriotic endeavors, entertaining troops abroad and assisting in the sale of $14 million in war bonds. He had been calling himself the "Groaner" for many years, but the grateful ser-

Young Bing

Bing around 1932

On the tennis court with wife Dixie Lee

*With his first family
in the late thirties*

vicemen called him Der Bingle.

An ardent sports fan all his life, Crosby's passion for golf is much heralded. He is also renowned for his charitable work—and golf and giving came together in 1936 when he founded the Bing Crosby Pro-Am Golf Tournament, with proceeds going to the needy. A devout Catholic, he has been conspicuously available for benefit performances for the Church.

In the 1940s, Bing moved into a mansion in L.A.'s Holmby Hills, where he led what many regarded as a dream existence, dividing his time between work, recreation and a large family. This placid life was tragically shattered in 1953, when Dixie died of cancer. It had long been rumored in the industry that she had helped Bing overcome his drinking problem, only to develop one of her own. Whether this was true or not, Bing's grief at her passing was certainly genuine. There were more problems in store for him with his sons, whom he had

*With his second family
on television in 1976*

evidently tried to raise with a combination of apathy and almost Victorian strictness, compelling them to work long hours for meager wages on his ranch in Nevada. When they were in their twenties, they formed a nightclub act, the Crosby Boys, and went on tour with it, trying to make up for their limited ability by exploiting their father's name. There were reports of brawls between the brothers, drunken horseplay, and professional negligence not unlike that of the young Bing. Two of the four married Las Vegas showgirls. "I think I failed them by giving them too much work and discipline," said Bing sadly. "Too much money and too little time and attention."

In 1957 Bing married Kathryn Grant, a beautiful young actress whom he had courted off and on for three years. Like Dixie, she gave up her career and began creating new Crosbys: Harry Lillis, Jr. (1958), Mary Frances (1959), and Nathaniel Patrick (1961). Bing wanted a new home to go to with his new family and moved to a $500,000 estate in Hillsborough, near San Francisco.

Crosby has been semi-retired since 1966, but he still does his annual television Christmas show (begun in 1935), now assisted by Kathryn and their three children. An abscessed lung brought him close to death in 1974, but he recovered, and in 1976 he toured the London Palladium, a Las Vegas nightspot, and a Broadway theater with a nostalgic fifty-year-anniversary show built around his career. In New York it was called *Bing on Broadway* and was billed as his "first New York appearance since 1931."

* * * * *

A Hollywood casting director once told Bing Crosby, "I don't think there'll be a chance for you in films—the ears are too wingy." When he married Dixie, a newspaper recorded the event: "20th Century-Fox Star Marries Obscure Crooner." For Bing, the years have provided a delicious revenge.

In a movie about Bing Crosby's life, one of the big scenes would have to be the crooner's first interview with Paul Whiteman, the man who is generally credited with having discovered Crosby. As Bing recalled it years later, the obese bandleader, clad in a luxurious black robe, was lounging in his dressing room at the Million Dollar Theater in Los Angeles, "looking like a giant Buddha." Quite unascetic, however, was the bottle of champagne on a nearby table and the dish of caviar on his lap. He was the picture of success, the most celebrated bandleader in the country, and when he offered Bing and his partner, Al Rinker, a job, the boys were jubilant.

They had crashed show business only a year before with the assistance of Al's sister, jazz singer Mildred Bailey. Billing themselves as "two boys with a piano . . . singing songs in their own way," they began to play small Los Angeles nightclubs. Their own "way" meant a jazzy, energetic style they called "hotcha." Soon they were touring the coast as part of a local vaudeville circuit. Their rise might not be termed meteoric, but it was certainly impressive. In October 1926, they cut their first record, "I've Got the Girl."

With Whiteman they quickly attained even greater heights, but with greater vicissitudes as well. Although Whiteman's band con-

THE ROAD TO HOLLYWOOD

tained such great jazz figures as Bix Beiderbecke, Joe Venuti, and Tommy Dorsey, Crosby and Rinker were by no means overmatched. Indeed, as the band toured Cleveland, Detroit, Pittsburgh, and other major American cities, the team from Spokane sang to one enthusiastic audience after another. Disaster struck at New York's Paramount Theater, however, where the crowd was cool to Crosby and Rinker—perhaps because the size of the theater made it hard to hear them.

Whatever the cause, the problem was not solved until singer-composer Harry Barris joined the group and the trio christened themselves with a new name, the Rhythm Boys. From this point on, the group's success was striking, including numerous engagements as part of the Whiteman band and a number of records, the best known of which is Barris' "Mississippi Mud." Unfortunately, Bing subverted the status of the Rhythm Boys by his dissolute and playboy-like behavior. Whiteman seems to have taken an avuncular posture with Bing, allowing the singer's boyish contrition and good-natured apologies to win reprieves. But when Crosby began missing shows, Whiteman banished the Rhythm

The Rhythm Boys: Al Rinker, Bing, Harry Barris

Boys to the provinces for an inglorious tour. Even there (or perhaps *especially* there), Crosby was undependable. Nevertheless, in 1930, when Whiteman was signed by Universal for *King of Jazz*, a film that was to be structured around him, the Rhythm Boys joined him in Hollywood. In fact, Bing was even assigned a solo number, "The Song of the Dawn."

But Crosby's errant tendencies undermined his opportunities again. Returning from a party in a rather tipsy state, he was involved in a traffic accident on Hollywood Boulevard and found himself jailed for a month for violating the Prohibition laws. After a week or so, Whiteman persuaded the court to let Crosby out during the day to

work on *King of Jazz*. By this time, "The Song of the Dawn" had been passed along to John Boles. Crosby was relegated to an ensemble number, "A Bench in the Park," which he and the Rhythm Boys performed with the Brox Sisters. Bing was heartbroken over losing his solo, but, in retrospect, "The Song of the Dawn" is a clumsy imitation of the Friml-Romberg school of operetta and could hardly have been crooned very effectively.

With neither success nor failure to show for his screen appearance, Bing went back on the road with Whiteman. His self-indulgent behavior had not diminished, however, and his innocent, blue-eyed penitence was growing ineffective. It was not long before Whiteman

The Crosby brothers: Bob, Bing, and Everett

Collegiate Bing

decided to find a more reliable vocalist. Crosby, Barris, and Rinker returned to the West Coast. They quickly established themselves at the popular Montmartre Café and then joined Gus Arnheim's band at the Coconut Grove.

By now Crosby's talent had matured even if he hadn't, and he emerged not only as the undisputed leader of the Rhythm Boys, but as a noteworthy local talent. He had a "sob" in his voice, people said, consciously or unconsciously echoing a similar paean to Al Jolson in *The Jazz Singer* ("I've heard a million jazz singers, but you've got a tear in your voice.") Soon Bing had a large, enthusiastic following in the Los Angeles area, and the "Crosby cry" was his trademark.

Despite Bing's cavalier approach to his career, he was, paradoxically, serious about his artistry from the beginning. He had schooled himself on Jolson from boyhood days, and while he was with Whiteman, he had had a chance to study a good Jolson imitator, Skin Young, who adopted Jolson's sob. Black jazz stylists had always fascinated him, and in between his own shows he often took a busman's holiday to see Duke Ellington and Louis Armstrong, from whom he learned the style of singing called "scatting." The records he and the Rhythm Boys made in the period 1927–1931—"My Kinda Love,"

"Till We Meet," "I Kiss Your Hand, Madame"—illustrate the swift development of Bing's distinctive singing style: a warm, husky tone; a precise but completely unaffected diction; a jaunty, easygoing manner; a number of vocal idiosyncrasies, such as whistling (also borrowed from Jolson), and the famous "boo-boo-boo" (his very own).

While entertaining nightly at the Grove, Bing had two insignificant flirtations with Hollywood. Duke Ellington persuaded the three Rhythm Boys to accept singing roles in his film *Check and Double Check* (1930), where they were given "Three Little Words." However, the film was edited in such a way that the song came out of the mouths of Ellington's musicians, and Crosby and his group were never seen. A few months later, the entire Gus Arnheim band, complete with the Rhythm Boys, was hired to appear in *Reaching for the Moon* (1930), a tale of shipboard romance with Douglas Fairbanks and Bebe Daniels. In one sequence, the passengers are entertained by Arnheim, Crosby and Co., who perform Irving Berlin's "When the Folks High Up Do the Mean Low Down." Next came *Confessions of a Co-ed* (1931), a collegiate soap opera in which Bing, Rinker, and Barris are cast as entertainers at a school dance.

25

Despite his popularity at the Grove, Crosby's negligence and carousing persisted, and eventually he ran afoul of the Grove's manager, Abe Frank, who docked his wages. Crosby left in a huff, thus occasioning two major developments: the Rhythm Boys split up, leaving Bing as a solo performer, and Frank saw to it that Crosby was blacklisted by the musicians' union.

Bing's older brother Everett, who had become his manager, saved the day. Through skillful promotion, he was able to land Bing a contract with Mack Sennett for a series of six musical comedy shorts, each twenty minutes in length and each paying $750. Instead of being allowed a specialty number or two in someone else's movie, Crosby himself would be the star, the aesthetic center. Each film was constructed around a song Bing had recorded: "Just One More Chance," "Wrap Your Troubles in Dreams," "I Surrender, Dear," "At Your Command," etc.

Although the silent comedy era was ended, Sennett was trying to transplant some of its slapstick traditions to the talkies—particularly those that had made him the King of Comedy. Although he discovered Chaplin and Keaton, cinematic perfectionists with an almost classical sense of order and symmetry, Sennett was himself improvisatory and cheerfully haphazard. A little romance, a lot of comic misunderstandings and pie-throwing buffoonery, then a climactic chase—these were the unvarying components of Sennett's work during the silent years. When he signed Bing, he was, of course, modifying his recipe, attempting to blend the Keystone brand of humor with the all-talking-all-singing-all-dancing shows that dominated the early sound era. Crosby, a romantic crooner whose fans were increasing every day, seemed likely to make an appealing and effective leading man.

The plot always involved Bing's attempts to transcend the obstacles that separated him from the lady of his heart. Once in a while, the gags were sophisticated enough to rest on obvious forms of mistaken identity; more often than not, however, they were burly, knockabout jokes in which someone put his foot in a laundry basket or disappeared into a vat of dough or fell into a fish pond. The climax was tried-and-true Sennett, a madcap chase sequence, with Bing and his girl pursued by policemen or the girl's parents or both.

Dream House, the fourth of these dizzy little opuses, is typical. It casts Bing as a plumber whose girl deserts him for a Hollywood career. He pursues her to the studio where she is shooting her latest film, some sort of Arabian nights monstrosity. Bing invades the set disguised as a

black extra ("Yowsa, yowsa," he cries, and it's all as tasteless as it sounds). To prevent the conceited hero of the Ali Baba epic from romancing his sweetheart, Crosby sings. The girl is entranced, as is the director, and all ends with music and reunited lovers.

Apart from their status as historical curios, the only pleasure the Sennett shorts can afford us today is listening to Bing sing some wonderful songs and watching him glide through the ponderous story material. As a performer he had always had comic impulses; he and Rinker had interlaced their songs with patter and horseplay from the beginning. Crosby had no trouble adapting to the requirements of screen comedy. His relaxed personality, innate sense of timing, and graceful, bemused gestures made him a natural for the screen. In the Sennett films, with their gaggle of vociferous caricatures, Bing seems like a gazelle among water buffalo.

The two major trade journals of the day, *Variety* and *Motion Picture Herald*, were divided as to Crosby's suitability for films. *Variety* hailed the arrival of a "marvelous new talent," while *Motion Picture Herald* found him lacking in "histrionic ability." The public agreed with *Variety*, and between March 1931 and September 1933 all six shorts were released.*

Shortly after completing his stint

With Bob Crosby (center) in a musical short

One of the early Sennett shorts
in ROAD TO HOLLYWOOD (1943)

with Sennett, Bing's career took off in a new direction. Everett had sent a copy of "I Surrender, Dear" to William Paley, head of CBS, and Paley, an able judge of talent, decided to test Crosby's radio appeal. In New York in the fall of 1931, the singer crooned to America over the airwaves and America loved it. He was immediately given a fifteen-minute spot five times a week, with Cremo Cigars picking up the tab. Next came a sensational engagement at the Paramount, where he had fizzled so badly a few years before that the manager had banished him from the stage. Now the theater was happy to pay him $7,500 a week for the duration of his engagement—seven months.

Almost overnight, Bing had become one of the biggest singing stars in the country, a performer who was equally magnetic on stage, records, or radio. Now all that remained was the conquest of Hollywood.

*Two postscripts must be added to the subject of Bing's movie apprenticeship. A sequence from *Dream House*, in which Crosby has a humorous set-to with a lion, was incorporated into *The Sound of Laughter* (1963), an anthology of old-time comedy. In 1943 an enterprising director named Bud Pollard reissued four of the Sennett films as *The Road to Hollywood*, purporting to trace Bing's early movie career. Unfortunately, Pollard fails to give his audience a clue as to the names and dates of the films; in addition, he throws the clips together so sloppily that it's hard to tell where one story leaves off and another begins. It all ends with an homage to Crosby that is so inflated it must have made even its subject blush.

29

K *ing of Jazz* is emblematic of the studios' early conception of a musical as a filmed vaudeville revue. These all-star variety shows, often drawing on the growing pool of radio talent, proved to be immensely popular for a time, and all the major studios were grinding them out. Between 1928 and 1931, audiences were "treated" to *The Hollywood Revue of 1929, On With the Show, Broadway Melody,* and countless others. Sometimes the only continuity in these pageants of performers was supplied by a master of ceremonies; other times there was a sparse plot that gave filmgoers a short breathing space between acts. Audiences soon tired of this "glorified vaudeville," which was largely static and giddy with the sound of its own voice. Not until *42nd Street* (1933), with its driving energy and its expert fusion of song and story, did the movie musical recapture its fans.

Nevertheless, Paramount perpetuated the revue show species in one form or another for almost twenty years. At their best, these films were legitimate musical comedies with definable plots; at their worst, they were throwbacks to the rudimentary version of the genre, loosely structured and top-heavy with stars. From the beginning of his long association with Paramount, Bing Crosby appeared in more than his share of these

VARIETY SHOWS AND CAMEOS

variety shows, and they are worth considering as a separate entity in his career.

Appropriately enough, Bing's first starring role in a feature film came in *The Big Broadcast* (1932), a movie which might just as well have been titled *"Paramount on the Air."* An affectionate poke at radio, *The Big Broadcast* kidded its infant rival but successfully hedged its bets by packing the movie with some of the top talent from the networks: George Burns and Gracie Allen, Cab Calloway, Arthur Tracy, etc. Of course, every movie of this sort needs a romantic lead, and what better choice than a crooner whose voice had set millions of feminine pulses aflutter on the radio and who had already demonstrated his screen potential? Bing was poised for stardom.

Loosely based on *Wild Waves*, William Manley's Broadway play of the same year, *The Big Broadcast* cleverly picked up where the Sennett films left off. As an ingratiating radio singer named Bing Hornsby, Crosby was not exactly cast against type. He loses his girl (Sharon Lynne), gets fired from his job, and goes out on a colossal bender; in a nightclub he joins mournful forces with another casualty of love, Leslie McWhinney

(Stuart Erwin). After an unsuccessful attempt at a double suicide, they decide to face life anew. As luck (and the necessities of the screenplay) would have it, McWhinney is a millionaire. He buys Hornsby's studio and puts the singer back on the air. The climax of the film is a national hook-up, and the necessary tension is provided by the question of whether Hornsby, who has disappeared, will show up or not.

The film got a generally friendly critical reception at the time of its release, though few reviewers saw any reason to hail the arrival of a major new screen star nor to characterize the movie as anything but a pleasant bit of musical froufrou. Stuart Erwin's comedic gifts and the array of big-gun radio talent impressed most reviewers more than Crosby's unemphatic charm and easygoing minstrelsy.

But, as so often happens, *The Big Broadcast* has improved with age. Seen today, it is an irresistibly entertaining work. The thirties radio station milieu, however frivolously it is treated, remains an interesting artifact of popular culture. The performers, too, are part of the history of the era, and each of them holds our interest: Kate Smith, the Mills Brothers, the Boswell Sisters, Vincent Lopez and his orchestra, Cab Calloway and his band, Donald Novis, and Arthur Tracy (The Singing Gypsy).

George Burns and Gracie Allen, who later distinguished themselves in nearly every medium, add their own sweet, crazy charm. Moreover, director Frank Tuttle shows that he had absorbed the disastrous lesson of the first phase of Hollywood musicals. Anticipating *42nd Street*, *The Big Broadcast* is all of a piece, and its pacing is unfailingly swift.

As for the pairing of Crosby and Erwin, it certainly does not work to Bing's disadvantage. Erwin's performance is a delight, but he is basically a gifted second banana. Crosby, on the other hand, not only has his singing voice and sufficient sex appeal to play leading men, he is an excellent light comic actor. Even at this early stage in his film career, he had cultivated the low-key mannerisms that were to make him a screen favorite for thirty years. The nonchalant shrug, the resigned little whistle, the ever-so-slightly-worried furrowing of the brow—these were the nimble gestures he had perfected in the Sennett films.

The Big Broadcast was also notable for demonstrating, at the very inception of Bing's film career, the remarkable extent to which his screen roles were shaped from his own experience. It's easy enough to say that Crosby played himself in *The Big Broadcast*—a radio crooner named Bing—but the autobiographical elements went deeper than this. After all, like the

MISSISSIPPI (1935). With Joan Bennett

man he is modeled on, Hornsby is a rather irresponsible figure, a bit of a drunk, a performer who doesn't always want to perform because he has a flippant attitude toward his career.

In terms of form, *The Big Broadcast* is additionally interesting, even arresting. Its moments of gay comic fantasy (e.g., telephone operators that sing, cats that walk in tune with clocks), though obviously derived from René Clair, are pleasing ornaments. In a darker vein, the "comic suicide" that Crosby and Erwin undertake—beneath a distorted hallucination of Arthur Tracy singing "Here Lies Love"—stands out as an early instance of black comedy, a few moments of home-grown American surrealism.

In 1935, in a distinctly sweet-and-sour combination, Crosby was teamed with W. C. Fields in *Mississippi*. What was intended as a dramatic contrast seems a bit more like incongruity today. At certain points, the misanthropic Fields and the melodious Crosby almost seem to be in different movies. Individually, however, they are in good form, and a film that is additionally embellished with a Rodgers and Hart score and a fetching antebellum setting can't be less than pleasing. Moreover, Crosby's Dumbo-esque ears had at last met their match in Fields' "great proboscis." (Less acceptable was Bing's unromantic girth, which had to be restrained by a girdle.)

Barely discernible in the plot were the remnants of Booth Tarkington's story "Magnolia," a satire on the dueling code of the Old South. The Quaker hero of "Magnolia" was reborn as Tom Grayson (Bing Crosby), a young Philadelphian whose plans of marrying into Kentucky aristocracy are aborted when he refuses to defend his fiancée's honor in a duel. Rebuffed by the family, he gets drunk and accidentally kills a man in a brawl. To escape imprisonment, he takes refuge on a showboat run by Commodore Jackson (W. C. Fields). There he becomes a singing star, the headliner of an assorted bill of dancers, jugglers, and comedians. Eventually his romantic attachment shifts from his fiancée (Gail Patrick) to her sister (Joan Bennett), and, after a suitable number of movie complications have been unraveled, the lovers are united and the family placated.

The parody in *Mississippi*, like that of *The Big Broadcast*, is all rubber arrows and blank cartridges; it's just a series of gentle digs at the crinolined customs and bewhiskered mores of a plantation society that seemed to be eternally "waiting for the *Robert E. Lee*." Essentially, the film is best viewed—and appraised—as a proscenium for Crosby and Fields.

The background of riverboat entertainment, with Crosby's fellow performers popping up at appropriate intervals, only serves to distance the movie from any real social satire and places it in the variety show category. Furthermore, Crosby's modern singing style is strictly an anachronism that wrenches the movie loose from its historical setting.

But as the agreeable diversion it was meant to be, *Mississippi* certainly holds up well. Crosby drifts amiably in and out of the crises that have been contrived for him. As for his vocal chores, he can hardly go wrong with the likes of "It's Easy to Remember," whose velvety elegance makes it ideal material for Crosby. The ironic mating of Bing's tranquil personality with a pistol-packing atmosphere is symbolized for us by Fields, when he drolly promotes Crosby as "Colonel Steele, the singing killer."

Paramount invaded radioland again in 1935 with *The Big Broadcast of 1936*. Interspersed with the featherweight story of a bankrupt radio station owner (Jack Oakie) was another variety show extravaganza, this time a parade of international performers headed by Crosby: tenor Richard Tauber, the Vienna Boys Choir, Amos 'n' Andy, etc. Director Norman Taurog relied much more heavily on guest appearances than Frank Tuttle had in the first *Big Broadcast*, and the antics of Oakie, broad as the day he left burlesque, are a descent from the brisker, more sophisticated comedy that Tuttle had provided for Crosby and Erwin. Here, reduced to a specialty number, Bing sings one song, "I Wished on the Moon," in a log cabin interior. The film did not do anything to advance Crosby's career, but it does serve as an illustration of the popularity he had attained in three years since his first major film. At the premiere, the audience applauded his number more enthusiastically than any of the others.

On loan to Universal, Bing got back into the center of things in *If I Had My Way* (1940), in which a nightclub provided the framework for the potpourri of songs, dances, and snappy patter. The screenplay concerned a couple of steelworkers (Crosby, El Brendel) who accompany an orphaned teenager (Gloria Jean) back east and encounter her jovial great-uncle (Charles Winninger). After being swindled out of the money they were supposed to keep in trust for her education, they wind up with a rundown New York bistro. But with performers like Blanche Ring and Eddie Leonard recreating the spirit of the Gay Nineties, the club is soon a flourishing enterprise.

If I Had My Way was probably inspired by Billy Rose's phenomenal success with the old-time vaudeville show he had booked into

MISSISSIPPI (1935). As Tom Grayson

his Diamond Horseshoe; it was a sell-out attraction for seventy weeks. Universal had a one-picture-a-year agreement with Crosby at this time, and they were clearly looking for a sure-fire vehicle. To the market-tested appeal of resurrected vaudevillians, the film added such ingredients as a Little Orphan Annie plot, El Brendel's Swedish-American stereotype, and the cornball populism that audiences had loved a few years before in *You Can't Take It With You* (snobbish, unfeeling rich people vs. the good-hearted poor).

But on the screen, even reinforced by Crosby's likeable presence, it all added up to very little. Ironically, the film returned the Crosby variety shows to their true origin, vaudeville, but it locked the revue material into a turgid story, easily the heaviest of any of the variety films. Seeking to provide its star with both comic and dramatic opportunities, it came up instead with silliness and sentimentality.

The following year, back at Paramount, Bing was much better served in *Birth of the Blues*. Instead of the usual random assortment of unrelated acts, this variety show had a built-in continuity. Each number was a virtual musical history lesson on the evolution of jazz. The story, dedicated to the "musical pioneers of Memphis and New Orleans who took music out of the rut and put it into the groove," was loosely derived from the experience of the Original Dixieland Jazz Band, a pioneering group of white musicians who exported black music to the North in the first quarter of this century.

As one might expect, the ambitious conception of *Birth of the Blues* was scaled down to the proportions of a stock movie musical. Growing up in New Orleans, clarinetist Jeff Lambert (Bing Crosby) becomes infatuated with the "colored people's music" and gives up the classical repertoire his father favors to become a jazz musician. He forms a small band, the featured member of which is a volatile cornet player named Memphis (Brian Donlevy), whom he finds in jail. Betty Lou Cobb (Mary Martin), a naïve young singer, joins the band, even though Lambert previously fleeced her in order to bail out Memphis. Over a period of time, the jazzmen soar to their predestined fame, while on the personal level a pitched battle goes on between Lambert and Memphis for the favors of Betty Lou. Lambert prevails.

On the racial level, *Birth of the Blues* requires a charitable attitude, a tolerance-in-reverse, since the movie is pretty thick-skinned about the theft of the black man's music by enterprising whites who knew how to make it pay. But judged as a slice of standard-issue entertainment, with solid musical

A 1936 publicity photograph, with Paramount starlets Eleanore Whitney and Marsha Hunt

IF I HAD MY WAY (1940). With Gloria Jean

values, the film is hugely enjoyable, nevertheless. The long series of jazz and blues classics are performed by no less than Jack Teagarden and his band, with some assistance late in the film from Louis Armstrong, Duke Ellington, and others. A black blues singer of the period, Ruby Elzy, gives a smoky and sensuous reading to "St. Louis Blues."

And let's not forget the stars. Whether their material is hot or cold, Crosby and Martin make the most of it. This is the early Mary Martin, after all, before Rodgers and Hammerstein had sanctified her in goo, and she's pure joy, especially when she "noodles" her way through "Waiting at the Church,"

a Johnny Mercer song written for the movie. Crosby has an ingenious sequence in which he entertains a theater audience of the day with "By the Light of the Silvery Moon" against a background of illustrated slides. In another sequence, he leads an impromptu jam session outside the jail where Donlevy, his cornet-player-to-be, is incarcerated.

Crosby headed his next Hollywood talent show in *Star-Spangled Rhythm* (1942), a twenty-one-gun salute to Paramount, with virtually every contract player on the lot doing his bit. This time the gems were strung on a plot line about a gatekeeper (Victor Moore), who is allowed to impersonate the president

BIRTH OF THE BLUES (1941), With Jack Teagarden and Eddie (Rochester) Anderson

BIRTH OF THE BLUES (1941).
With Mary Martin and Brian Donlevy

of the studio in order to impress his son (Eddie Bracken), a visiting sailor who thinks Dad is a big-shot. The plot thins rather than thickens, and by the end the entire Paramount studio finds itself pledged to entertain the crew of Bracken's ship, which makes for a boffo wind-up, of course.

Bing appears with his nine-year-old son Gary in tow to do an indifferent skit with Betty Hutton. He also leads the huge ensemble number, "Old Glory," that concludes the show with suitably star-spangled fervor. To be kind about it, it was 1942 and the U.S. had several million men under arms. Besides which, as one observer put it, Crosby's patriotism was "the most graceful flag-waving of the year."

Bing's next film was *Dixie* (1943), a "biopic" with marked similarities to his revue-style movies. The life of composer Dan Emmett, who created the Virginia Minstrels, it was structured around various minstrel show acts. There were no guest appearances in this one, but the constant intrusion of Mr. Tambo and Mr. Bones, of interlocutors and sidemen, amounted to a series of specialty acts.

This was the old Hollywood, in which biographical truth was always subordinate to the needs of the story and the fanciful ideas of the screenwriters. Scenarists Karl Tunberg and Darrell Ware went to work on Emmett's life, and by the time they got through with it, they had a story about a young musician who leaves home with $500 and dreams of glory. He is fleeced by a conman named Bones (Billy De Wolfe), who then has a change of heart and guides Emmett into show business. Soon the two have founded the Virginia Minstrels, who popularize burnt-cork entertainment. (The blackface element in *Dixie* makes it one of the few controversial Crosby films: many race-conscious television stations refuse to show it). All the while, Emmett has been forgetting about his sweetheart back home (Marjorie Reynolds) and falling under the spell of a sexy boardinghouse proprietor (Dorothy Lamour).

When he introduces his big number, "Dixie," the audience is indifferent at first because the tempo is too slow. With fortunate negligence, Emmett has accidentally started a fire, however, and must accelerate his song to hold the audience's attention. The romantic conflicts in the story are cleared up when Emmett's old girl is crippled

STAR-SPANGLED RHYTHM (1942). Bing sings "Old Glory."

for life and he loyally returns to her side. In this, his first color film, we are for the first time able to see Bing's blue eyes as clearly as the heroine.

Like *Birth of the Blues*, *Dixie* spurns the jagged truths and disorderly episodes of real life in favor of a pat and predictable story. In actuality, the film is more intriguing as another retelling of the Bing Crosby story: a portrait of the artist as an engaging, naïve, and very careless young man. Perhaps *careless* is too mild a word; in the course of the movie, Crosby—with the aid of his trusty pipe—is responsible for burning down three separate vaudeville houses. He doesn't strive too hard for success, but, with a combination of luck, happenstance, and general ability, he attains it anyway.

In addition to Emmett's work, the film contains Stephen Foster's "Swanee River," which Bing performs memorably. Otherwise, it is the lively series of minstrel show scenes that energizes the movie and keeps it moving along. Indeed, it positively struts when the interlocutor announces, "Gentlemen, be seated!" and the frock-coated Mr. Tambo and Mr. Bones take the stage. The antique comedy routines, walkabouts, and cakewalks are lovingly—and expertly—recreated.

The scene of Bing's next variety show anthology was laid in the

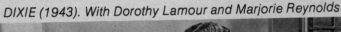

DIXIE (1943). With Dorothy Lamour and Marjorie Reynolds

DIXIE (1943). Leading the minstrel show.

most famous dive of the day, "Duffy's Tavern" in Brooklyn. The popular radio show of the same name, a favorite of millions in the forties, featured Ed Gardner as Archie, the gabby, malapropian bartender. When Archie's story took to the screen in 1945 in a film entitled (surprise) *Duffy's Tavern*, it proved to be a sentimental yarn about a down-and-out business-man trying to put his bankrupt record company back in operation. There's only one thing that can save the hero's neck in a Paramount film of this genre: everybody on the lot.

Led by Bing Crosby, they once again go loyally on parade—Betty Hutton, Alan Ladd, Paulette Goddard, etc. And once again the grab-bag is a mixture of gold and dross. Bing's scene, in which Robert Benchley presents a funny chronicle of Bing's rise for the benefit of the four Crosby boys, is the gold.

In *Variety Girl* (1947), Bing was back in front of a brigade of Paramount celebrities. Occasionally, the film takes time out from its floor show to advance a sketchy tale about a young stage-struck girl who is sent to Hollywood by the Variety Club, a real-life philanthropic organization that had been active since 1928. By the end of the film, the Paramount stars must shine again—this time in a benefit show for the Variety Club. Somewhere in the Mardi Gras of performers, the world's most famous crooner can be glimpsed with his sometime partner, Bob Hope. They feud their way affectionately through a duet called "Harmony."

When *Mr. Music* opened in 1950, Bosley Crowther welcomed back "our old friend Bing Crosby" in a part that "fit him—and he it—like a glove." No one could dispute that assessment in a film which cast the crooner as a Broadway songwriter who would rather play golf than piano and who is more interested in bookies than backers. Conflict enters in the person of Charles Coburn, a down-at-the-heels entrepreneur who wants a new show from Crosby and dispatches a stern young assistant (Nancy Olson) to see that it gets written.

The musical is a refurbished treatment of Samson Raphaelson's play, *Accent on Youth*, in the form of a backstage musical, and it's even closer to pure effervescence than the original. *Mr. Music* bubbles along its predetermined course, with a specialty number

VARIETY GIRL (1947). With Bob Hope and William Demarest

MR. MUSIC (1950). With Groucho Marx

THE GREATEST SHOW ON EARTH (1952). With Bob Hope

spotted here and there, and climaxes in the "big show," which has been in preparation all along. Crosby does a sketch and song with Groucho Marx; the Merry Macs sing; Crosby and Dorothy Kirsten do a mock face-off of popular music and opera; Marge and Gower Champion hoof energetically; Peggy Lee joins Bing for another duet. It's a shame they don't have a better score to work with. The Burke-Van Heusen efforts sound all too much like the work of a man who spent most of his time playing golf. Director Richard Haydn knows what to do with the material in *Mr. Music* and the movie

floats serenely along, but perhaps more in the manner of a dirigible than a balloon.

Mr. Music did not make beautiful music at the box office, and Bing blamed it on the title, which, he said, made him sound like a know-it-all: "That . . . title took in too much territory for anybody, especially me, since I know relatively little about music."

To the list of variety shows in which Bing was seen only in cameo must be added an indeterminate number of voiceovers in cartoons and feature films, narration assignments, and unbilled cameos.

Bing did his first voiceover quite

unwittingly in *Check and Double Check*, but when his familiar pipes were borrowed again it was under very different circumstances. In Paramount's *Out of This World* (1945), Eddie Bracken played a homely, unprepossessing messenger boy who stuns the entertainment business with his incongruously mellow singing voice. There was probably no one in America who was in doubt as to whom the voice actually belonged, but Bracken acknowledged the famous source at the end of the film by remarking to the camera, "Thanks, Bing."

Audiences seemed to find it easy to settle back and listen to Uncle Bing tell them a story or two in his restful tones, so Walt Disney hired him to narrate the "Ichabod Crane" segment of *The Adventures of Ichabod and Mr. Toad* (1949). In 1966 he was again a disembodied voice in *Cinerama's Russian Adventure*, an overblown travelogue of the Soviet Union that figured in one of our cultural exchange programs with the Soviets.

Crosby's best-known cameos are those he did with Bob Hope in Hope's own vehicles; these quick, uncredited spots became a kind of running gag. In *The Princess and The Pirate* (1942), he surfaces in the last scene to snatch the heroine (Virginia Mayo) from Hope; in *Son of Paleface* (1952), he is glimpsed driving away from the studio, while Hope reassures us, "I guarantee this fellow won't be in the picture tonight"; in *Alias Jesse James* (1959), he plays an unnamed gunslinger who comes to Hope's aid in the final shoot-out, commenting, "This boy needs all the help he can get." He can also be spotted briefly in *My Favorite Blonde* (1942) and *My Favorite Brunette* (1947). Together with Hope, Bing is a readily discernible but unidentified member of the audience in *The Greatest Show on Earth* (1952).

In 1960 Bing had two cameo roles for which he received screen credits: *Let's Make Love*, a dreary romantic comedy with Yves Montand and Marilyn Monroe, and *Pepe*, Hollywood's disastrous attempt at selling Mexican comic Cantinflas to American audiences. In the former, Bing and Gene Kelly, playing themselves, are hired by billionaire Montand to give him singing and dancing lessons. In the latter, Crosby is one of the crushing multitude of film stars that envelope Pepe when he goes to work for a Hollywood director.

As a cameo performer, Crosby's duties in these films were light, but, if *Duffy's Tavern* is any indication, his paycheck was pretty heavy. He got $26,000 for that one.

The majority of Crosby's films are unpretentious musical comedies that feature his voice, his wit, his imperturbable charm. Bigger than Rudy and before Frank, Bing was already established as the best of the big-time crooners when Hollywood beckoned a second time. Paramount's executives gave him a chance—flappy ears and all—because they had turned down Gable and, certainly, outsized ears had never stood in *his* way. The studio soon discovered that it wasn't just his voice on records and radio that caused women to swoon. He was a male Clara Bow, the "It" guy. Over the next forty years, Paramount took "It" to the limit. They dressed their star up as a sailor, a big-band singer, a college boy, a cattle rancher—and they made the same picture over and over again.

The agreeable little plots are suitable setups for Bing's songs. The girls are pretty. People fall in love, have some laughs, and shed only a few tears. The resulting confection is iced with the lighthearted touch that is Bing's own brand of comedy. These Crosby films are pure fun that move quickly through ninety minutes of escape. They ask nothing but to entertain.

There were many years, especially in the thirties, when Bing strolled through two or three of these pleasingly innocuous movies. In 1933, for example, his fans got to see *College Humor, Too Much*

CROONING, SPOONING, AND SPOOFING

Harmony, and *Going Hollywood*.

College Humor was directed by Wesley Ruggles, who was later to extend Bing's range in the offbeat *Sing You Sinners* (1938). In its satire of the college films of the twenties, *College Humor* affords a glimpse of the sophistication that would surface as the director and his star matured. Otherwise, it is a pat Crosby vehicle. Bing is a drama professor who finds himself involved in the lives—or should we say love lives?—of three of his students. The girl that one of these students has his eye on happens to have developed a crush on her professor. (Need we guess which professor?) The spurned suitor also happens to be one-half of Mid-West University's winning duo on the football team; the other half is the starry-eyed coed's brother. These two clowns get so tangled up in their romantic problems that Mid-West barely wins the big game against Eastern College, which is the climax of the fun.

Jack Oakie and Richard Arlen are delightful as the collegiate cut-ups, and Mary Carlisle throws herself at her unsuspecting prof with sweet innocence and an arsenal of musical talent. The songs by Sam Coslow and Arthur Johnston include "The Old Ox Road," a charming takeoff on West Point's Flirtation Walk. The college humor turns to hilarity when George Burns and Gracie Allen appear (all too briefly) as a couple of crazy caterers.

The critical reaction to *College Humor* could hardly be called earthshaking; it was generally regarded as adequate fluff. Although a new, highly professional Bing demanded take after take, the old Bing went out on a binge and interfered somewhat with the picture's shooting schedule. Nevertheless, he came out with his best notices to date. One reviewer, revealing a hint of former skepticism, wrote, "Mr. Crosby turns out to have a sense of humor and his subterranean blue notes are easy to listen to."

Too Much Harmony capitalizes on another popular film subject of the time—the backstage romance. The screenplay was written by none other than young Joseph L. Mankiewicz, many years before he became the celebrated writer-director-producer. It is a song-filled show, once more with music and lyrics by Coslow and Johnston.

Despite its title, there's a great deal of discord behind the curtain. Bing, as a handsome songster, is going with one girl (Lilyan Tashman) and in love with another (Ju-

COLLEGE HUMOR (1933).
With Richard Arlen (in white sweater)

TOO MUCH HARMONY (1933). With Judith Allen

dith Allen). True love triumphs, but only after some helpful shenanigans by Jack Oakie, Skeets Gallagher, and Kitty Kelly. The cast, which also includes Ned Sparks, Billy Bevan, and Mrs. Evelyn Oakie as son Jack's stage mother, is suitably enlivened under Edward Sutherland's direction. However, no one is as genuinely funny as Harry Green, who plays theatrical producer Max Merlin. Without the occasional spark of Green's comic energy, the show is only mildly amusing. Certainly Bing was not at his best. Perhaps he was a little too relaxed by the undemanding na-

ture of these films, or perhaps he was just tired. At any rate, the reviewers were not kind. The *New York Times* critic noted that his acting was "often apt to make one uneasy." He even turned against the crooning, denouncing "Crosby's peculiar ballads."

Going Hollywood made amends. MGM borrowed Bing for this Marion Davies showcase—at $2,000 a week! The studio also substituted Paramount's more intimate tradition in place of its own musical extravagance. Although William Randolph Hearst financed the project at great cost, the extravagance

GOING HOLLYWOOD (1933). With Marion Davies

was *off* the set. Miss Davies held sumptuous three-hour lunches in her regal quarters, retained a band to set the mood by playing popular songs of the day, and invited the cast and crew for Roman weekends at San Simeon. Director Raoul Walsh was somehow able to finish the film in between the long and frequent intermissions for dancing, eating, and other gaiety.

The story by Frances Marion and the lovely little melodies of Nacio Brown and Arthur Freed come together nicely under Walsh's control. The contributions of Bing and Miss Davies are enhanced by top-notch support from Fifi D'Orsay, Ned Sparks, Stuart Erwin, and Patsy Kelly, who stepped off the Broadway stage for her first role in a full-length film.

As the movie opens, everyone is "going Hollywood." Bing and Fifi D'Orsay are stars and sweethearts on their way to make a movie together. Miss Davies, a kindly and unassuming schoolteacher, is a lovesick fan, sufficiently enamored of the crooner to follow him on his way west. By the time they've reached the coast, she's captured both Bing's heart and the volatile Miss D'Orsay's part.

Going Hollywood pumped adrenalin into Marion Davies' wilting career. It also put Bing into box office "Top Ten" charts. It was Miss Davies who was astute enough to insist upon signing Bing, over the objections of Hearst, who disliked Crosby's singing. Fortunately for all concerned, she exercised her unusual persuasive powers over the newspaper magnate. Oddly enough, if we consider Bing's merry reputation, it is the sullen "Temptation"—a drunken tribute to the absent teacher, sung in a Mexican bar—that is the highlight of his performance. It was his first serious song on film.

In 1934, in another three-picture year, Bing and Paramount made *We're Not Dressing, She Loves Me Not*, and *Here Is My Heart*. First place among Bing's light musical comedies goes to the richly entertaining *We're Not Dressing*. This film's similarities to Lina Wertmuller's *Swept Away* seem astounding if one is unaware that both efforts are based loosely on Sir James Barrie's play *The Admirable Crichton*. Anticipating Giancarlo Giannini, Bing even knocks co-star Carole Lombard around a few times.

Of course, *We're Not Dressing* adds music to the Barrie story: the humble sailor croons while he fishes for food and melts the aristocratic defenses of Doris Worthington (Lombard). There's also some excellent comedy, provided by Ethel Merman and Leon Errol as two of the guests on the Worthington yacht, and by George Burns and Gracie Allen as scientists on the other side of the island who carry

WE'RE NOT DRESSING (1934). With Carole Lombard

on their research with side-splitting wackiness.

However, the dark overtones of class and sex struggle that are emphasized by Wertmuller are unmistakably present here, too. It is the lowly sailor, not the film's imperious patricians, who knows how to survive when the Worthington yacht is capsized. It is the self-sufficient plebe who becomes king of the remote island on which they're all stranded. Even the film's hit tune, "Love Thy Neighbor," can be seen to have sociopolitical overtones.

Unlike *Swept Away, We're Not Dressing* backs down at the end. Bing turns out to be an architect who has followed the romantic call of the sea before throwing himself into his career. Once his social status has been righted, Miss Worthington can marry him with a clear conscience.

Bing had first met Lombard a few years earlier when she was dating his public rival and private friend, Russ Columbo. Now she was dating Clark Gable. Crosby and Lombard hit it off famously, but director Norman Taurog had his share of problems with the earthy blonde. Not only did her lack of inhibitions shock the residents of Catalina Island, where the film was made, but she went wild at one point and attacked Bing. She had an irrational fear of being hit

SHE LOVES ME NOT (1934). On the set with Miriam Hopkins and director Elliott Nugent

HERE IS MY HEART (1934). With Kitty Carlisle

and, in the scene that called for Bing to slap her she slapped her co-star back, knocked him to the ground, and tore off his toupée. Bing recovered but refused to repeat the experience. The fight is retained in the final print. If we watch carefully, we can see the very real horror on the faces of the cast as they witness her unexpected outburst.

She Loves Me Not and *Here Is My Heart* both feature Kitty Carlisle as Bing's romantic interest. According to Ms. Carlisle, the affection ended when the cameras were turned off. She is one of many celebrities who have complained about Bing's distant professionalism; hence, the well-known reputation for coldness that is rivaled by his reputation for charm.

She Loves Me Not is a fast-paced frolic about a Princeton student who gets mixed up with a nightclub dancer and the gangsters who are chasing her. It is somewhat disconnected as it races back and forth between the Princeton campus, a nightclub in Philadelphia, and a movie studio in New York; still, if we can hang on, it's worth it. Miriam Hopkins is unforgettable as the bawdy broad who causes all the trouble, as is Lynne Overman, the studio publicity man who wants to capitalize on her plight.

Although he was thirty-three, Bing passes well as a Princeton man. Kitty Carlisle, as a dean's daughter, looks and acts a little too sophisticated for an undergraduate. Still, her throaty, semioperatic voice goes beautifully with Bing's. The musical collaboration of Mack Gordon, Harry Revel, Ralph Rainger, and Leo Robin produced several more-than-pleasant melodies, among them "Love in Bloom." (Rainger and Robin would go on, this time with Lewis Gensler, to give us "June in January" for *Here Is My Heart*. These two songs were Bing's first major film hits.) As a result of director Elliott Nugent's talent for farce, *She Loves Me Not* walked away with flattering comparisons to the venerable *Charley's Aunt*, another collegiate caper. One other note: this was the last film in which Bing allowed Paramount to glue his famous ears back, a cosmetic device which the studio had insisted upon from the beginning. The heat from the lighting on the set caused them to pop out intermittently, and he finally insisted they stay that way. Consequently, *She Loves Me Not* presents Bing's ears in a variety of inconsistent proportions.

Here Is My Heart, a second film adaptation of the French play, *The Grand Duchess and the Waiter*, contained two additional tunes that became well-known: "Love Is Just Around the Corner" and "With Every Breath I Take." Bing plays J. Paul Jones, a famous crooner who

TWO FOR TONIGHT (1935). With Mary Boland

retires from the stage to do all the things he's ever wanted, including falling in love with a real live princess. Finding the United States in short supply of royalty, he goes to Monte Carlo where, sure enough, he finds Princess Alexandra (Kitty Carlisle). The arrogant young woman is so shielded from the hoi polloi that Bing has trouble getting close enough to her to accomplish his mission.

Here Is My Heart won raves and deserved them. Crosby, Carlisle, and Reginald Owen (as a member of Alexandra's entourage) are par-ticularly good. Carlisle projects a natural haughtiness which appears to make her more comfortable as a princess than a dean's young daughter. As for Bing, his perform-ances generally vary only with the amount of fun he seems to be hav-ing. It's obvious here that he's hav-ing a wonderful time, fulfilling his character's fantasies and poking fun at royal pretensions.

Bing slowed down in 1935 and produced only one film in this gen-re, *Two for Tonight*. The second half of this movie slows down also, leav-ing bland memories, which are per-

RHYTHM ON THE RANGE (1936). With Martha Raye (center). and other cast principals, including an unknown Roy Rogers at extreme left

haps not fair to the movie as a whole. Actually, this little film about a family of songwriting sons gets off to a grand start. As one of Mary Boland's three boys, Bing has to make good his mother's claims that he's a playwright by delivering the book of a musical in seven days. "A play only lasts two hours and you've got a whole week to write it in," she tells her appalled son.

He succeeds in delivering the libretto but only after a self-consciously serious quest for dramatic material. Fortunately, Lynne Overman is back and proves to be as funny a producer as he was a publicity man. Bing boo-boo-boos

along, but neither he nor Overman can save the movie from its progressive deterioration. In addition to the lugubrious second half, there is a notably unfunny performance by co-star Joan Bennett and a thoroughly undistinguished score. Director Frank Tuttle, usually Paramount's first choice for a Crosby film, gets the credit for *Here Is My Heart* and the blame for *Two for Tonight.*

Rhythm on the Range (1936) and *Rhythm on the River* (1940) are charming exercises in miniaturism. Both films are deceptively modest—our appreciation comes as we realize with what dexterity they've been drawn to scale.

In *Rhythm on the Range*, Bing plays a cattle rancher who comes to New York for a rodeo at Madison Square Garden. On his way back west, he discovers a runaway heiress (Frances Farmer) in the nicely furnished boxcar he shares with his prize bull Cuddles. The young lady in turn discovers she likes cactus better than skyscrapers. Bing's not thrilled with the idea at first (Crosby is often initially cool in his films, letting the ladies win *his* heart), but finally the two are united for an old-fashioned Western wedding.

Although it's unintentional, there's plenty of humor in casting Bing as a cowboy. Even though he milks cows and rides steers and croons to Cuddles, he's a pretty sophisticated cowboy, almost a Ragtime Cowboy Joe. But we soon suspend our disbelief and he becomes just as credible a cowpuncher as a priest.

Rhythm on the Range gave a start to young Johnny Mercer, whose "I'm an Old Cowhand" became a hit. The film is particularly notable, however, for introducing Martha Raye—and she enters to gales of laughter. Audiences responded gleefully to her grotesquely comic appearance and raucous style. (In addition, if we look quickly, we can see Roy Rogers playing guitar as part of a frontier band.)

In *Rhythm On The River*, Bing has been hired, along with Mary Martin, as a ghost-writer for a fa-

RHYTHM ON THE RIVER (1940). With Mary Martin, Oscar Levant, and Basil Rathbone

PENNIES FROM HEAVEN (1936). With Edith Fellows,
Louis Armstrong, and Donald Meek

mous composer (Basil Rathbone). The two unknowns meet coincidentally and fall in love. They write a song, "Only Forever," which they vow to keep to themselves. When they discover that they also write for the same composer, they try to combine their talents and break into the business. They have a rough time until they reluctantly surrender "Only Forever," which puts them forever on top.

Rhythm on the Range and *Rhythm on the River* have good music, good casts, good comedy. Although both are unpretentious films, they somehow seem better in their total effect than larger pictures that claim to be great.

In addition to *Rhythm on the Range*, Columbia, borrowing Bing from Paramount, released *Pennies From Heaven* in 1936. Although the show was regarded as one of his best, only the song survives.

Crosby plays a remarkably well-groomed wandering minstrel whose dreams of singing his way down the canals in Venice as a gondolier are interrupted by a destitute "family"—a ten-year-old child (Edith Fellows), her feeble grandfather

WAIKIKI WEDDING (1937). With Martha Raye
and Bob Burns

(Donald Meek), and the social worker (Madge Evans) assigned to their case. Reluctantly, Bing finally adopts them all.

The comedy and music in *Pennies From Heaven* are submerged by its all-pervasive but graceful sentimentality. The film owes its acclaim less to Bing's contribution than to the performance of Fellows, who guilelessly manipulates our heartstrings.

While visiting Hawaii with Dixie in 1936, Bing heard bandleader Harry Owens sing a touching tribute to his daughter, "Sweet Leilani." After convincing Owens to let him use it in *Waikiki Wedding*

(then in production), Bing had to threaten to abandon the picture before producer Arthur Hornblow would agree to use the song. Crosby felt strongly about the number, and he was right. "Sweet Leilani" won the Oscar for the Best Song of 1936.

Outside of Martha Raye and radio monologist Bob Burns, whose lanky Will Rogers frame and droll delivery had received attention in *Rhythm on the Range*, there is little else of note about *Waikiki Wedding*. Bing plays a public relations man who must convince America's Miss Pineapple Girl (Shirley Ross) that her first prize, a trip to Hawaii,

DOCTOR RHYTHM (1938). With Mary Carlisle, Laura Hope Crews, and Beatrice Lillie

PARIS HONEYMOON (1939). With Franciska Gaal

EAST SIDE OF HEAVEN (1939). With Baby Sandy and Joan Blondell

is truly a trip to a tropical paradise. After a little romancing by the blue waters, she needs no more convincing. The audience, however, remains unconvinced that the cast and crew of this strictly Hollywood production—with its American "natives" and synthetic hulas (choreographed by LeRoy Prinz) —ever set foot on Hawaiian shores.

Doctor Rhythm (1938) displays an impressive list of stars and supporting players on its masthead—including Mary Carlisle, Bea Lillie, Andy Devine, and Sterling Holloway. More loosely than it claims, this film is adapted from the O. Henry story, "The Badge of Policeman O'Roon." *This* version is about a crooner and the annual police show—two little items that O'Henry never dreamed of.

Whatever its title connotes, *Doctor Rhythm* goes more and more for laughs than for music. Sometimes its search for a titter becomes a little desperate; despite its we're - all-having-a-ball-at-the-party-and-we-hope-you-are-too atmosphere (at one point, Lady Bea even winks into the camera), we still feel uninvited.

THE STAR MAKER (1939). With Louise Campbell

Of course, it's almost worth attending this boring function to hear Bea Lillie perform her department store routine in which she keeps garbling her request for "two dozen double-damask dinner napkins . . . ."

Paris Honeymoon (1939) was another tiresome effort. Bing is again a cowboy; this time he's so rich that he has left the range completely behind—except for his ten-gallon hat. He goes to Paris and falls in love with a divorced heiress (Shirley Ross) and then leaves her behind in Paris to have a fling with a Ruritanian peasant (Franciska Gaal).

The names behind the scenes are readily identifiable as Paramount's Crosby regulars: Frank Butler, Don Hartman, Leo Robin, Ralph Rainger, and, of course, Frank Tuttle. The team became a little too relaxed about turning out another Crosby vehicle. It's a ho-hum attempt to capitalize on a success formula. Ho-hum or not, *Paris Honeymoon*, like all of these pictures, made money. Still, even Bing's unruffled attitude was no asset here. As Bosley Crowther put it in *The New York Times*, "One thing about Bing, you never catch him acting. He is always himself." And, in this case, Bing can't disguise the fact that he is bored.

Waikiki Wedding, *Doctor Rhythm*, and *Paris Honeymoon* suggest that the stencil Paramount seemed to be using for Bing's movies was getting a little faded. Universal replaced it with *East Side of Heaven* (1939). Crosby is in good form here and is admirably supported by Joan Blondell and Mischa Auer. The real star, however, is Sandy, an 11-month-old baby beginning a brief reign as Universal's child star. Bing gets involved in a King Solomon struggle over the baby between the child's wealthy and autocratic grandfather (C. Aubrey Smith) and his mother (Irene Hervey).

In the movie's best scene, Hervey has kidnapped Sandy from her father and has asked Bing to hide the baby in his apartment. A pajama-clad Crosby nervously walks the floor holding the little bundle gingerly in his arms. To quiet Sandy, he tries crooning. The famous singing style seems to have the same effect on infants that it has on older feminine "babies."

Bing does not bear the burden of his temporary fatherhood alone, however. He receives wholehearted support in his troubles with Sandy from his roommate (Mischa Auer) and his fiancée (Joan Blondell).

Auer and Blondell also share the show's profusion of good gags and attractive songs.

East Side of Heaven remains what it was in 1939, a nice way to spend an afternoon. Bing and babies are proven crowd pleasers. Together, they see to it that the cup of entertainment almost runneth over.

If one baby had worked so well for Universal, Paramount felt it should try a truckload of tots. *The Star Maker*, which was released in August of that year, was inspired by the life of vaudeville promoter Gus Edwards, whose all-children revues had turned out, among others, Eddie Cantor, George Jessel, Walter Winchell, and Mervyn LeRoy. In making the film, Paramount duplicated Edwards' talent for recruiting underaged ability, displaying these dimpled discoveries in the midst of an account of its impresario-hero's many headaches.

Except for its rather pedantic discussion of child labor laws, the story is worth telling, even in highly fictionalized form. As the film opens, Larry Earl (Bing), a struggling songwriter, is at the piano wooing a lovely lady (Louise Campbell), while brightening the sad little eyes in the orphanage where she works. Later, as his wife, Mrs. Earl struggles to make do while her determined husband pursues his dream. There's no break until he sees a group of ragged

HERE COME THE WAVES (1944). With Betty Hutton

newsboys hoofing for nickels on the street. He sets their heels tapping to his music and, with a little ingenious, although implausible, help from his wife, gets the country's biggest promoter to give them a chance.

Those newsboys turn into million-dollar babies. With an endless supply of stage mothers and a promotion train that takes Earl's child auditions into the hinterland, he's set for life—until recently enacted legislation in the area of child employment closes the show. Meanwhile, some of his discoveries have grown up and gone on, without a backward glance in his now poverty-stricken direction. But Earl always has an eye on the future, and we know he'll come out all right. The movie ends with his marveling over a "radio," a new and disdainfully received invention. He gets a gleam in his eye, and we can almost see the symbolic lightbulb going on over his head —the same one that lit up when he first saw those newsboys many years before.

Bing is excellent as the struggling entrepreneur, and Louise Campbell is a most pleasing leading lady. Ned Sparks, as Earl's public relations man, "Speed" King, gives us a fresh dose of his inimitable dry comedy. Sadly enough, the kids are what's wrong

RIDING HIGH (1950). With Clarence Muse and Coleen Gray

with *The Star Maker*. Although fourteen-year-old Linda Ware, who sings with the Los Angeles Philharmonic (Walter Damrosch conducting), is truly remarkable (as are many of the other children), so much talent is unnatural in the hands of babes. It is almost as if we are being asked to witness a carnival freak show.

While Der Bingle was helping the armed forces by selling war bonds and entertaining the troops, he was capitalizing on the war effort for those left at home. In *Here Come the Waves* (1944), he plays a sailor whose waves are not the oceanic variety but twin sisters (Betty Hutton) who look alike but have personalities that are polar opposites—vivacious and sedate. One of his fellow shipmates (Sonny Tufts) has a claim on one of the twins. The problem is, which one is Susie and which one is Rosemary? We see where the comedy comes in, and the score by Harold Arlen and Johnny Mercer (the best of which is "Accentuate the Positive") is woven skillfully into a WAVE recruiting show.

There is, of course, the predictable military message—Uncle Sam Wants *You*—this time carried out through scenes of WAVES in training. *Here Come the Waves* is, however, good old-fashioned Crosby, reminiscent in its richness of his earlier fare. We all know Betty Hutton can play live wires, but here she gives a fine comic sedation to the part of the dignified twin.

Moving into its third decade, the "Crosby film" was going stronger than ever with Frank Capra now taking his turn in the director's chair. The Crosby/Capra team made two enormously successful efforts in the light musical comedy genre: *Riding High* (1950) and *Here Comes the Groom* (1951).

For Bing, the only thing better than sitting around a racetrack was owning a horse (he started his stable in 1935), or even his own track (he and producer Hal Roach founded the Santa Anita Racetrack). The next best thing was to play horse-trainer and owner Dan Brooks in *Riding High*—the remake of Capra's sixteen-year-old *Broadway Bill*.

Once Capra had reined in the well-known Crosby casualness with regard to shooting schedules (if Crosby wasn't there on time, he would simply start shooting without him), the director got along famously with his star. And Bing got obvious pleasure out of making this movie and more than held this own, despite a strong cast which included Coleen Gray, Charles Bickford, Frances Gifford, William Demarest, Oliver Hardy, *and*, from the earlier film, Raymond Walburn, Clarence Muse, Ward Bond, and Paul Harvey.

There were few differences in the two scripts, and absolutely no

*HERE COMES THE GROOM (1951). Bing leads the cast
in "Mr. Cristofo Columbo."*

HIGH TIME (1960). With Nicole Maurey

attempt was made to fit Crosby into the character Warner Baxter had played in *Broadway Bill*. Nevertheless, Bing added his own personality, which, probably due to the material, has never been more fun-loving or expansive. Brooks is delightfully easygoing about everything but his horse. He even gives up an heiress to concentrate on his beloved nag's racing career. You can imagine how he feels when he has to bury the most important thing in his life. We sniffle rather than bawl, because Capra and Crosby avoid turning this moment into mush. *Riding High*, with its vigorous racetrack ambiance and warm moments, is a winner.

On the surface, *Here Comes the Groom* bears a marked resemblance to *Little Boy Lost*, made two years later. Crosby is a reporter abroad who brings home two French children (Jacky Gencel and Beverly Washburn) orphaned by the war. The similarities end when our star, who must marry within five days to provide a suitable home in the eyes of the American authorities, chooses a woman (Jane Wyman) who is already about to be married to someone else. Her fiancé (Franchot Tone) is, among other things, more athletic, wiser, and much, *much* richer than her new suitor. But, undismayed, Bing proves he's more ingenious—and, in doing so, more disarming—than just about anyone.

Here Comes the Groom is nicely garnished with an imaginative performance of a great song. Capra had been criticized for his handling of the music in his films, but Bing credits his innovative staging of "In the Cool, Cool, Cool of the Evening" with bagging the Academy Award. The song had been in the trunk since Johnny Mercer and Hoagy Carmichael had written it for an extinct Betty Hutton project. It is an unusually mobile number, with Bing and Jane starting the song in an office and continuing with it through the hall, down the elevator, and out onto the street—all in one take! In addition to Louis Armstrong's playing, Phil Harris' croaking, and Bing's and Dorothy Lamour's entertaining a planeful of passengers with "Mr. Cristofo Columbo," the film introduces Anna Maria Alberghetti performing "Caro Nome" from *Rigoletto*.

With this film as an index, it's not hard to see why Bing has his sights set on Jane, whom Capra aptly summed up in the single phrase—"short nose, long legs, big heart, and all talent." When the five-day deadline is reached, we're happy to see Franchot Tone realize that Alexis Smith is more suitable to his Brahmin tastes. That leaves Miss Wyman free to say, "Here comes the groom, . . ." along, of course, with the two French children who started it all.

Bing's crooning, spooning, and spoofing ended where it had begun—on campus. There's an even greater irony: in *College Humor* (1933), Bing played a professor, whereas in *High Time* (1960) he's a student! Paramount has been replaced by 20th Century-Fox, Bing has exchanged his raccoon coat and ukulele for a simple sweater and slacks, and the dorm is filled with sounds of rock-and-roll instead of jazz; still, it is the same old University of Hollywood and Vine!

As Harvey Howard, Bing is a middle-aged man who had made enough millions to endow libraries. Now he wants to *enter* them and chooses the stacks at Pinehurst U. In only a few years the football games and fraternities depicted here would be as dated as the elegance of Princeton's rooms in *She Loves Me Not*. No one knew it, however—especially Howard, who enthusiastically attends the school's football games, with their bonfire-lit rallies and pompon-waving cheerleaders, and survives the hazing of Xi Delta Pi. He also does some apple-polishing with a pretty French professor (Nicole Maurey).

As fellow students, Tuesday Weld and Fabian seem better suited to high school. The real pity of this movie, however, is that Bing is fifty-nine. His weariness and worn visage fail to bring the script to life. This mediocre property could only have survived in the early days when its star's powerful presence was enough. By now, the crooner had even been superseded as the country's number one singing idol. It is symbolic that Frank, not Bing, made a hit out of the show's big song, "The Second Time Around." Perhaps Sinatra's earthier rendition seemed more provocative to the jaded tastes of a new era than the fundamental innocence of Crosby's interpretation. At any rate, it was high time for him to turn to other things.

Paramount's musicals were seldom as opulent or imaginative as the ones Fred Astaire and Ginger Rogers did at RKO and Busby Berkeley staged at Warner Brothers. Occasionally, however, Paramount did copy the more exquisite musical originals that came out of the costlier houses. Elaborate production numbers, scores by Gershwin or Porter, partners like Astaire were added to complement Bing's light, casual touch and informal style. His film personality did not grow or expand with his budgets, and yet the new elements never seemed inharmonious. A vast chorus line of pretty girls enhances Bing's melodies.

Broadway's biggest hit in 1934 (420 performances) was the bouncy, tuneful, irreverent musical *Anything Goes* with its classic Cole Porter score ("Anything Goes," "I Get a Kick Out of You," "You're the Top"). Paramount's decision in 1936 to bring *Anything Goes* to the screen, starring Crosby, was certainly an auspicious beginning for the entry of both the studio and its star into more extravagant musicals.

The screenplay is largely faithful to the zany P.G. Wodehouse-Guy Bolton-Howard Lindsay book. Billy Crocker, a Wall Street businessman (Crosby), accidentally winds up on an ocean liner bound for England, along with nightclub singer Reno Sweeney (Ethel Mer-

ELABORATE ENTERTAINMENT

man, recreating her Broadway role) and Moonface Martin (Charles Ruggles), a gangster who is disguised as a minister. Crocker is smitten with a fourth passenger —Hope Harcourt (Ida Lupino). It seems to him that Hope is the unwilling companion of some dangerous-looking men; in reality, she's a runaway heiress being returned to England by private detectives.

Once on board, Crocker realizes that he has no clothing, no passport, and no room. Because the good "reverend" takes a liking to him, he solves Billy's problems by bequeathing him the stateroom and passport of his original traveling companion, Snake-Eyes Johnson, who has failed to show. Inevitably, Crocker is mistaken for Johnson, who is Public Enemy Number One. As the show moves along, Crocker pursues Hope while the ship's officers pursue him. After the liner reaches British shores, this complicated web is untangled: Crocker's true identity is established, Moonface is demoted to "not dangerous and not wanted," and the characters are left to continue their shipboard romances.

Lewis Milestone, who had distinguished himself with the classic war film *All Quiet on the Western*

Front, seems like an odd choice as director. Superficially, he did a commendable job of duplicating the Broadway show. Both the story and the best-known of Porter's songs are kept intact. However, some studio genius added a hodgepodge of forgettable numbers by Leo Robin and others. The lavish "Chinese" production number that was appended at the end of the film is an embarrassment. Despite lush costumes, beautiful girls, and Ethel Merman, it seems disjointed and amateurish. In all fairness, a suave nightclub number that Paramount inserted is splashy and effective. The sequence features Merman belting out "I Get a Kick Out of You," while sitting in a gold ring that floats around the club.

The replacement of Victor Moore—who played Martin on the stage but was unavailable for the movie—with Ruggles was understandably lamented by many critics. On the other hand, despite one complaint that Bing crooned "You're the Top" with no sense of its comic edge, no one seemed to miss William Gaxton, the original Billy. Crosby's performance has the same light-comic gift that marked his earlier films. Merman performs with her customary, leather-lunged zeal.

For all of its bright spots, *Anything Goes* is, on balance, disappointing. In spite of the pretested material, Paramount's adaptation serves only to confirm its limitations in the musical arena. We expect more inventively staged musical numbers and more ambitious choreography from such a major show. *Anything Goes* comes to life only fitfully, and usually on individual merit rather than as a well-executed whole.

Looking back from the seventies, we find only two additional points of interest. Like the stage version, *Anything Goes* contains some surprisingly wicked moments that shed light on the morals of the period. In the less racy years that followed, for example, the line "Some get a kick from cocaine" from Porter's song was changed to "Some like the perfume from Spain." Also, on a more contemporary note, Moonface Martin's traveling alias is the Reverend Dr. Moon!

Double or Nothing (1937) is not exactly a big Bing musical, nor is it his standard fare. Still, the movie contains two of the best and most expensive production numbers in the entire Paramount/Crosby repertoire. Bing Crosby and Martha Raye worked so well together in *Rhythm on the Range* the previous year that Paramount decided to pair them again. Each was so enormously popular that when the movie opened at New York's Paramount Theatre on September 1, 1937, 3,000 people were standing in line by 10:00 A.M.

ANYTHING GOES (1936). With Ethel Merman

ANYTHING GOES (1936). With Ida Lupino

Double or Nothing contains one of the most offbeat and provocative plots that ever served to string a score together. Bing is an indigent singer; Martha, a former stripper; William Frawley, a conman; and Andy Devine, a simple-minded hobo named "Half-Pint." All find wallets containing $100 bills. They return them to the address printed inside and are told that the wallets were left in accordance with the will of the late Axel Clark.

Clark has used his will to settle a long-standing dispute with his brother Jonathan over whether man is innately both honest and intelli-gent. If Clark won, the honest and intelligent men who helped him make his postmortem point would inherit his estate. If all candidates failed, the money would go to the already sizeable bank account of his brother. By returning the money, our four main characters prove their honesty. The movie revolves around their attempts to prove their business savvy. As stipulated in the will, they are each to double their $5,000 reward by legitimate means. The first to do so wins $1,000,000.

Despite the fact that nearly all of our characters try to double their

DOUBLE OR NOTHING (1937). With Walter Kingsford, Andy Devine, Martha Raye, and William Frawley

Singing with Martha Raye

HOLIDAY INN (1942). With Fred Astaire

money in a way that is musically entertaining, *Double or Nothing* is filled with dark sociopolitical overtones. The sardonic Jonathan has an equally evil wife and two spoiled children. Each tries to win the trust of one of the subjects in the experiment and steer him or her toward bad investments. The most easily tempted is conman Frawley who, in a fine dramatic scene, tells Jonathan that this is his only opportunity to go straight. Unaffected, Clark persuades him to buy worthless silver certificates. Our characters finally get wise, pool their remaining resources and win the million, but it's touch and go all the way.

Bing also wins the daughter. In one of the most extravagant production numbers in Paramount's history, he moves his nightclub—the investment that doubles the money—to another location (by means of electronic walls and floor) moments before Clark, who secretly holds the mortgage, is about to close the club on a building technicality. The club comes apart and leaves Jonathan in his bare warehouse as his daughter dances and sings a triumphant good-bye with Crosby and his friends.

Before the final jamboree in the nightclub, we have been entertained by Bing's singing and danc-

HOLIDAY INN (1942). With Marjorie Reynolds

ing (five numbers), the dance teams of Ames and Arno and the Calgary Brothers, and two sensational numbers by Martha Raye. Raye performs a witty satire of the burlesque profession called "It's On, It's Off" and is featured with a bevy of beauties wearing scant sailor jackets in a spectacular moonlit production number; it takes place on the bows of rowboats floating in the Central Park lake.

For all of its worth, *Double or Nothing* collects dust in film libraries. Not so with Irving Berlin's *Holiday Inn*, which is undoubtedly

Crosby's most famous musical. The film has become traditional television fare during the holidays, largely because of the nostalgically familiar moment when Bing sings "White Christmas" to Marjorie Reynolds while the snow swirls outside his cozy New England inn.

Berlin conceived *Holiday Inn* and, while Claude Binyon and Elmer Rice were developing his idea, wrote thirteen melodies to match the American holidays around which his story revolves. With these songs and its serviceable plot (one fraught with romantic rivalries and disappointments), *Holiday Inn* is a quintessential musical. It is a feast of sparkling musical episodes served up at holidays, each holiday presented to us as a perfect rendering of picture-postcard Americana.

Appropriately, by 1942, when *Holiday Inn* was released, its star had become as much of an American symbol as Thanksgiving turkey. Bing had by then appeared in thirty-four movies and seemed to have permanently captured first place at the box office. Only Fred Astaire could equal Bing's effortless talent, and Paramount brought them together here to complement Berlin's lilting score.

The pair play two-thirds of a successful nightclub act that is broken up when Jim Hardy (Bing), an easygoing type who might even be called lazy, retires to a farmhouse in Connecticut. There he opens up a nightclub which, to insure his relaxed modus vivendi, is open only on holidays. His sophisticated ex-partner, Ted Hanover (Astaire), has a proven record in stealing Hardy's girls. He has already broken up Jim's engagement to the fickle lady who made up the remaining third of the act. Now, thrown over by the vamp and looking for a new dancing partner,

BLUE SKIES (1946). Bing leads the singing and dancing chorus in "Cuba."

BLUE SKIES (1946). With Fred Astaire

he shows up at Jim's place and once again threatens Hardy's romantic security. Jim has fallen for a starstruck young dancer, Linda Mason (Marjorie Reynolds). He decides to fight for her, but his deceitful methods drive her into Ted's arms. Together they dance off to Hollywood and are almost at the altar when Jim shows up. Linda hears him sing "White Christmas," and we know where her true feelings lie.

Linda wasn't the only one who reacted strongly to hearing Bing sing "White Christmas." When Berlin first presented the song to producer-director Mark Sandrich, he said quietly, "I have an amusing little number here." That "amusing little number" turned out to be the most successful song ever written. To date, over a hundred million copies of the record have been sold, thirty million of them by Bing. Crosby initially refused to sing or record "White Christmas." Fortunately, his prescient recording manager, Jack Kapp, persuaded him that he would not be capitalizing on a religious holiday. Due to the singer's lingering resistance, the recording session took only sixteen minutes.

The world was at war, and "White Christmas" took on special meaning for the troops stationed far from home. Crosby recalls, "I sang it many times in Europe in the field for the soldiers. They'd holler for it; they'd demand it and I'd sing it and they'd all cry. It was really sad."

Not to be outdone by the success of "White Christmas," Fred Astaire created his own records with *Holiday Inn*. His dance sequence, "Say It with Firecrackers," the Fourth of July number, is said to be the fastest dancing in movie history. It's hard to gauge such a claim but not the genius of the choreography in which Astaire sets off firecrackers by throwing them on the dance floor or kicking them off in perfect rhythm with his tapping. The number took thirty-eight takes and three days to shoot.

He creates another of the film's great moments when, on Valentine's Day, he dances to Berlin's lovely "Be Careful, It's My Heart" with Marjorie Reynolds. They dance silhouetted behind an enormous red satin heart. Suddenly, they leap through the heart onto the dance floor and continue their romantic whirling without a missed beat. Both alone and in partnership with Reynolds and Virginia Dale, Astaire did so much vigorous dancing in *Holiday Inn* that he went from 140 to 126 pounds by the end of the picture.

As if all this weren't enough, Bing peeks under Miss Reynolds' new bonnet one spring morning and woos her with "Easter Parade." They're riding in a carriage through the Connecticut countryside instead of strolling down Fifth Avenue, but we don't mind. Because of such scenes, *Holiday Inn* can be likened to a series of Norman Rockwell paintings, its reassuring idealizations as warming to the spirit as roasted chestnuts and an open fire.

Bing Crosby, Fred Astaire, and Irving Berlin joined together in 1946 with equally successful results. The occasion was *Blue Skies*, again based on an idea by Berlin, adapted by Allan Scott and Arthur Sheekman. With more than twenty Berlin songs, the movie is a fine tribute to his music. Once more we have two song-and-dance men vying for the hand of a beautiful young woman. And Joan Caulfield, as the center of their attentions, *is* almost ethereally beautiful, especially when exquisitely clothed by Edith Head. But she is also so listless that it's hard to believe she is the reason for all the singing, dancing, and squabbling.

The story, worn as it is, has a new touch. This is one of the few Crosby musicals where we do not have to wait until the end to see him get the girl. He marries Joan while the picture is still comparatively young; however, this deviation is superficial. As a happy-go-lucky but successful nightclub owner (again!) who can't stay in the same nightclub or the same business for more than a year, he divorces Caulfield as soon as she objects to his lifestyle. Then we have to wait until the end of the film for him to get her

back. Not unexpectedly, Astaire again loses his love to Bing at the altar. Here, however, he loses her not once but *twice*. As in *Holiday Inn*, he puts his hands in his pockets, shrugs, and stays friendly.

Blue Skies has its share of melodrama. After some time, Bing visits his daughter unannounced. She no longer recognizes him. Astaire, hitting the bottle in frustration over Miss Caulfield, falls from a high platform during a production number and never dances again. There are also some speeches about a wife's role as equal business partner and decision-maker that would bring nods of approval from today's women's libbers.

Above all, *Blue Skies* has music, music, music. Astaire announced that this would be his last picture and, as a fitting good-bye, gives his fans some dazzling dancing to "Putting on the Ritz." In striped pants and top hat, he works a magical syncopation with his tap shoes and his cane, while trick photography backs him up with a chorus line of dancing self-images. The climactic production number during which Astaire is injured is none other than "Heat Wave"; beside Astaire's rendition all previous or later performances pale.

Bing, no stranger to his role as ingratiating vagabond, seems more sober than we've seen him before. Still, he underplays the melodrama of the serious moments admirably.

THE EMPEROR WALTZ (1948). With Joan Fontaine

THE EMPEROR WALTZ (1948). With Joan Fontaine

In fact, his acting is the best in the movie. When necessary, he hoofs (quite competently!) with Astaire. Elsewhere he cuts up with his sidekick, Billy De Wolfe. He's even so attractively romantic that we can see why Miss Caulfield never recovers from his first kiss. But most of all, he sings Berlin—"Blue Skies," "Cuba," and "You Keep Coming Back Like a Song," a lovely ballad that is introduced in the film and became a hit. After hearing Crosby's mournful and foreboding interpretation of the title song, we will never want to hear "Blue Skies" without the depth that his clouds have added.

Special mention should go to Billy De Wolfe for the laughs he generates. As Tony, he follows his employer and friend, Crosby, from one nightclub venture to the next —from the "Flapjack" to the "Songbook" to the "Top Hat" and so on. We're grateful that he never gets so sick of being uprooted that he leaves the picture. The sensual Olga San Juan is Tony's female counterpart. She hangs around on the periphery, singing with Bing and dancing with Fred, and we love every moment of her performance.

Crosby followed *Blue Skies* with

two films which, although obviously expensive and certainly entertaining, provide very little in the way of music, good or otherwise. *The Emperor Waltz*, released in 1948, contains only three songs —and two of those were already familiar! With a scanty plot to boot, it's hard to believe that our interest can be maintained. There's no need to worry, however, thanks to an exceptionally winning performance by Bing and some of the wittiest dialogue this side of the Danube by Billy Wilder, who directed and co-authored the screenplay.

Bing's fine mood may have resulted from his concurrent negotiations to buy the Pittsburgh Pirates—an investment which would thrust him into the front office of his favorite spectator sport. Whatever the reason, he is thoroughly engaging as Virgil Smith, an American salesman who has come hawking his wares at the palace door of the Emperor Franz Joseph. The "wares" in this case are "new-fangled phonographs," and Smith's canine companion, Buttons, looks remarkably like the dog in the RCA Victor trademark.

Our fast-tongued friend talks the sweet emperor out of a sizeable portion of his royal annuity in exchange for the record players. He also croons a countess into love with him, while, at the same time, her aristocratic French poodle,

A CONNECTICUT YANKEE IN KING ARTHUR'S COURT (1949).
With William Bendix

Scheherazade, is very much taken with his mongrel. Just when everything seems like an Austrian version of the American dream, Franz Joseph refuses to countenance all matches made with commoners—both men and dogs. All ends well in this tale of "the love affair that rocked Vienna." Scheherazade, although the wife of the royal black poodle, gives birth to a litter of miniature Buttonses, while the proud owners waltz their way back to Newark with the old emperor's blessing.

Buttons' similarity to Victor's listening dog is only one instance of a script jam-packed with tongue-in-cheek hilarity. While Bing is waiting to see the emperor, his phonograph falls over and the needle skims the surface, resulting in a clicking that sounds ominously like a bomb. When it attracts the attention of the courtiers, who think it's an assassination attempt, Bing proudly points at his merchandise and says casually, "This is gonna kill him." When they appear appalled by his remark, he naïvely leans over and whispers, as if in further explanation, "He'll be in sections." The laughs in the film, however, are mainly at the expense of European class distinctions.

Although this breathtaking movie was shot in Canada, the white-tipped mountains and black-green forests are convincingly alpine. The palaces, the summer homes, the satin gowns re-create the luxury of another era. Despite the dearth of music—the best of the songs is Bing's adroit attempt at yodeling "Friendly Mountains" —*The Emperor Waltz* is a marzipanlike confection fit for royalty.

Richard Haydn's likeable emperor is almost eclipsed by the numerous pleasantries of *The Emperor Waltz*. On the other hand, Sir Cedric Hardwicke's endearing King Arthur is almost the only virtue in *A Connecticut Yankee in King Arthur's Court* (1949). Released only a year apart, the movies are as similar in tone as they are dissimilar in quality. Both pictures are romantic farces, short on music and long on nonsense. The court of the Round Table has been reproduced with the same sort of Technicolored attention to detail that marked its predecessor. And not the least of the similarities is that both of our royal personages are continuously troubled by worrisome colds (a disadvantage of living in drafty palaces). *The Emperor Waltz*, however, had Joan Fontaine. *Connecticut Yankee* features Rhonda Fleming as Lady Marian, an unfortunate choice that takes the picture from the sublime to the ridiculous. We want to groan rather than laugh when Rhonda blinks wide, maidenly eyes and speaks in Hollywood's version of "Auld English."

As the Yankee, Bing does his best to save the show, admirably supported by a dryly funny Hardwicke and clownish William Bendix (who shows how wide-eyed innocence and antiquated English are supposed to work). When the three team up for "Busy Doing Nothing," they provide the high point of the movie.

Oddly enough, this particular version of Mark Twain's 1889 novel has been overrated in many quarters. What with the liabilities of Ms. Fleming, a screenplay by Edmund Beloin which is much too coy in its attempts to be contemporary, and the uninspired direction of Tay Garnett, audiences would do far better to see the 1921 silent version or the 1931 talkie with (sorry, Bing) Will Rogers.

Anything Goes and *Holiday Inn* became such standards that each was subjected to a remake. In 1956, twenty years after the original, the second *Anything Goes* premiered. Confronted by two movies with identical titles, television executives changed the first *Anything Goes* to *Tops Is the Limit*, the title by which it is currently distributed. In the updated production, Bing co-starred with Donald O'Connor, Mitzi Gaynor, Phil Harris, and French ballerina Jeanmaire. Sidney Sheldon devised a new story and screenplay; Paramount, how-

ANYTHING GOES (1956). With Jeanmaire

WHITE CHRISTMAS (1954). With Rosemary Clooney

WHITE CHRISTMAS (1954). With Danny Kaye

ever, continued to credit the original writers—although certainly not for any contributions their work lent to the newer version. And once more Cole Porter's shoulders were not deemed broad enough to carry the musical side of the show on his own. Jimmy Van Heusen and Sammy Cahn were hired to come up with three new songs; any three old Porter songs picked at random would have been better.

Twenty years wrought only three improvements: VistaVision, color, and the choreography of Roland Petit and Ernie Flatt. To its detriment, the original *Anything Goes* contained very little dancing to Porter's melodies. Petit and Flatt blended the considerable and varied talents of O'Connor, Gaynor, and Jeanmaire with exciting results.

As one critic observed, the plot is new but not fresh. Bing is a musical-comedy star who goes to Europe on a vacation with his aggressive young opposite number in television (Donald O'Connor). The two want to mix a little business with pleasure by finding a new leading lady for an upcoming show. They find not one, but two, suitable young women (one for each of them, or course). Bing and Donald don't see the neat symmetry at first. Over the course of the picture, they must work their way out of what seems to be a jam and achieve a happy ending.

Now grown, O'Connor still looked exactly as he did eighteen years before when, at the age of twelve, he had played Bing's kid brother in *Sing You Sinners*. This time, however, he was aware of the league he was in. The crooner had to depart from his customary coolness in order to warm up his awed and somewhat paralyzed co-star. O'Connor was surprised that Bing was able to hoof so well. In the singing department, O'Connor's attempts to croon like the master brought a sly observation from Danny Kaye. "Why is it that when they make a picture with Bing, they all sound like Crosby?" he quipped.

Anything Goes 1956 is only one or two degrees more unsatisfying than *Anything Goes* 1936. Despite the carbonation of two supremely talented casts—and, in the earlier instance, a good book to boot—both efforts remain disappointingly flat.

Paramount's remake of *Anything Goes* may have been sparked by the dazzling success two years earlier of *White Christmas*. Despite its pale comparison to *Holiday Inn*, this film was, like its title song, one of the biggest money-makers in Bing's career.

Bing co-produced the venture with Paramount and Irving Berlin. Even at sixty-eight, Berlin was so thrilled to get back to work that he wrote eleven new songs, among them "Count Your Blessings" and

HIGH SOCIETY (1956). With Grace Kelly

*HIGH SOCIETY (1956). With John Lund,
Grace Kelly, and Frank Sinatra*

"The Best Things Happen While You're Dancing." He hung nervously around the set and became especially anxiety-ridden when it came time for Bing to record "White Christmas," which appears at the beginning and at the end of the movie. "You know," Bing reassured Berlin, "I did record it a long time ago—I really know the song."

Critics were generally unsympathetic to *White Christmas*. At least Berlin was not arraigned for the show's basic failings. Reviewers blamed director Michael Curtiz and screenwriters Norman Krasna, Norman Panama, and Melvin Frank for placing a major-league original in a minor-league park. Only Bing and his co-stars—Danny Kaye, Rosemary Clooney, and Vera-Ellen—escaped the critics' harsh words.

Although it was turned into a ski lodge, the New England inn of the original survives the remake, and, unfortunately, resembles its cherished predecessor. However, in the new story the inn is not particularly profitable, and our song-and-dance men (teamed up with a singing sister act) bring it back to life rather than buying it. Over the Christmas holidays, they put their friends in the rooms upstairs and each other on stage to show their appreciation for the owner, whom they admired when he was their commanding officer during the war.

We understand (and, in retrospect, are amused by) the heavy-handed patriotic sequences of *Holiday Inn* and *Blue Skies*. We were at war, and at some point each film sounds an earnest call-to-arms amidst the music. But *White Christmas*, made long after the war was over, contains no fewer than *three* rousing numbers in tribute to army life. Either the studio hoped to capitalize on the original reaction of military men to "White Christmas" or, as one writer suggested in what could be a thinly disguised reference to Bing, "someone's nostalgia for the war years and the U.S.O. tours has taken the show awry."

White Christmas, beset by minor problems throughout shooting and unfavorable notices after its release, is nevertheless worth seeing. Dean Jagger is appealing in the overexposed role of the general. Danny Kaye, who took over the part of Bing's sidekick after Fred Astaire and Donald O'Connor turned it down (Astaire didn't like the script and O'Connor had back

problems) proves yet another compatible Crosby co-star. Bing and Rosemary Clooney make equally good love and music together. It is a technically beautiful film, Paramount's first in its wide-screen process of VistaVision and Technicolor. And, finally, with all the high-priced gourmet ingredients, how can the soufflé taste all that bad?

The last time Bing made big music was in 1956 with *High Society*, a remake of Philip Barry's *The Philadelphia Story* with songs. It was the first time the two most renowned crooners, Crosby and Sinatra, appeared together, and co-star Grace Kelly compared their good-natured oneupsmanship on and off the set to Crosby's more famous friendship with Bob Hope.

High Society is in the high style of MGM. It is a strictly upper-crust production that copies handsomely the affluent life it portrays. In addition to its glamorous stars, the studio spent money to simulate the haughty habitats of Newport (moved from Philadelphia), to design the chichi costumes of Paris and New York, and, fittingly, to provide the additional elegance of a Cole Porter score.

Since Barry's story concerns the indecision of a socialite over the three men in her life—her over-starched fiancé, her ex-husband, and a journalist—the female role that Katharine Hepburn had made famous in 1940 was vitally important. The studio decided to choose the nearest they had to Hepburn: the well-bred, Philadelphia-born Grace Kelly.

Bing and Miss Kelly had become close friends in 1954 with *The Country Girl*, and he was delighted that he would be playing her ex-husband. He even pressed MGM to let her sing their "True Love" duet, rather than hiring a behind-the-scenes vocalist. Miss Kelly is still grateful that both she and the studio reluctantly acquiesced. The duet resulted in her first and only Gold Record and Bing's twentieth. Since its release, "True Love" has earned her over $50,000 in royalties—a fitting reminder of the last film she made before becoming a princess.

Unfortunately, the Cole Porter hit is the only memorable moment in Grace Kelly's performance. Her debutante background is her one real asset in this film. Though she probably ranked higher on the social scale than Hepburn, her sedate and brittle loveliness was a poor substitute for the eccentric, tomboyish flair of her predecessor. Without Hepburn, the Barry story—even set to music—just isn't as much fun.

Either producer Sol C. Siegel and director Charles Walters had never glimpsed fashionable society or they didn't care about credibility. Bing is also miscast. Not only does he seem too old for such romantic silliness, but he is misnamed as C. K. Dexter-Haven and out of place in the Social Register world that he supposedly inhabits. Tuxedoed stuffiness hardly goes with Bing's pipe, buttoned-down cardigan, and alpine hat.

The pleasure in *High Society* is merely intermittent. Sinatra and Kelly work up a nice chemistry in an amusing sequence that has Sinatra fishing for spicy revelations about society. Two generations of crooning come together, along with two of the most famous pairs of blue eyes in the world, when Bing and Frank team up for a musical dissertation on drawing room mores, "Well, Did You Evah?"* And, needless to say, Louis Armstrong holds his own as a black Peter Duchin, Satchmo-style. A fine supporting cast, which includes John Lund as the fiancé and Celeste Holm as a sardonic photographer, does its best to fulfill the playwright's original intentions.

---

*The two singers joined forces one more time, in *Robin and the 7 Hoods* (1964), a self-consciously cute fable about Frank and his seven friends, who, although ostensibly gangsters, emulate the Merry Men of Sherwood Forest. Playing dramatically (and ludicrously) against type, Bing is Allen A. Dale, a stuffed shirt who persuades the gang to turn some of their illicit wealth over to charity. The bad plot and dialogue are compounded by even worse songs, and one of Bing's numbers, "Don't Be A Do-Badder," is possibly the low point of his career.

Bing Crosby once said to Don Hartman, who, with Frank Butler, wrote the scripts for the first three "Road" films, "If you hear one of your lines, yell Bingo!" The road that Crosby and Hope traveled over a period of twenty-two years led to the Hollywood version of seven exotic locations: Singapore, Zanzibar, Morocco, Utopia, Rio, Bali, and Hong Kong. It didn't matter that the scripts were practically interchangeable. It didn't matter that the means by which the two zany heroes unwittingly found themselves searching for Alaskan gold mines, being launched in moon rockets, or braving charging rhinos on African safari were only sketchily explained. It didn't even matter whether their breathtaking escapes from cannibals, deserts, blizzards, jealous lovers, and marauding gangs were even semi-plausible. The "Road" pictures, without attempting to make sense, made millions. They delighted audiences and critics alike, created a new genre of improvisational crazy comedies, and—until James Bond came along—made more money than any series of films in movie history.

In the late thirties, a number of South Sea Island escape films helped American audiences forget war clouds abroad and a Depression at home. In 1939, Paramount decided to make its own series of such films. The premise was sim-

BING, BOB, AND DOROTHY

ple: a pair of lovable characters would romp through escapades and narrow escapes in remote settings. The studio hired Hartman and Butler to write *Road to Mandalay* and offered the leads to Jack Oakie and Fred MacMurray. When Oakie and MacMurray turned them down, Paramount decided to pair Burns and Allen with Crosby, their biggest star. Bing said yes, but Burns and Allen, who are on record as having found Crosby rather cold, weren't interested.

From the first, Paramount's logical choice should have been to team Bing with Bob Hope. In 1939, Crosby and Hope were hosting the two most successful radio shows in the country. They had first met in 1932, when they were on the same bill at New York's Capitol Theatre. When they weren't performing, they hung out across the street at O'Reilly's Bar, drinking, playing pool, and honing their incisive comedic talents on each other for the benefit of O'Reilly's patrons.

By 1939, the two were back at each other's throats, this time to the delight of their radio audiences. Crosby would have Hope on his show and kid him about his "ski-slope nose." When it was Hope's turn, he'd introduce Crosby as "a

Clowning with Bob Hope off the set

fat little singer." And worse. Paramount finally decided to set them loose on each other, counting that their particular brand of biting jest would work on the screen as well as it did over the air.

Another ingredient of the "Road" series, as initially envisioned, was a girl for the "feuding twosome" to fight over. The studio chose a former Miss New Orleans, Dorothy Lamour, whose dusky sensuality had already made her a fixture in movies with tropical locales. It was not as important to Paramount's executives that Miss Lamour could sing or act (she was passable in these departments) as that she looked exceptionally good in a sarong.

This native vision was certain to have a jealous boyfriend who would cause further problems for the unendingly beleaguered American bumblers. A young actor named Anthony Quinn, whose swarthy, muscular good looks subtly threatened ferocious retaliation if he were crossed, won the part. Ironically, Quinn, still a minor film actor at the time, was earning $2.00 a night impersonating Bing Crosby at private parties.

Somewhere along the line, *Mandalay* became *Singapore*. Songwriters Johnny Burke and James V. Monaco and director Victor Schertzinger (who was also a composer) came up with a romantic tune for Bing to croon to Dorothy;

a plaintive solo for Dorothy, lovesick over Bing, to sing to the moon; a couple of lively duets for Bing to perform with Bob; and an elaborately choreographed and heavily populated native dance. Hope and Crosby hired their own gag writer, Barney Dean, to liven up the script. Although Dean worked for both performers, *Road to Singapore* began a tradition in all seven "Road" pictures: Hope got the lines; Crosby got the girl. With surprisingly few changes, the formula outlined in Paramount's initial conception—the talent utilized, the structure, the tone—was to last from Singapore to Hong Kong.

Road to Singapore was shot in four months and released in the spring of 1940. It proved successful beyond even Paramount's carefully calculated projections. *Singapore*, based on a story by Harry Hervey, was the most structured of the "Road" pictures and contained a minimum of the ad-libbing and asides to the audience that came to characterize the series.

Josh Mallon (Crosby) is heir to a wealthy shipping fortune. He feels stifled by the insistence of his family and fiancée ("one of the 0's in the 400") that he fit into a white shirt by day, a black tie by night, and a wedding ring. His seafaring sidekick, Ace Lannigan (Hope), has his own set of problems —namely, the shotgun-toting father and brothers of an innocent

ROAD TO SINGAPORE (1940). With Gloria Franklin,
Dorothy Lamour, and Monte Blue

that they think Lannigan has spoil-ed and then scorned. Ace and Josh decide to take definite steps to pre-serve their carefree lifestyle before it's too late: they set sail for the most remote reaches they can find, solemnly swearing off women for-ever.

We next see them, low on funds (a frequent problem), in a charm-ing shack in Kaigoon. But financial reverses never stop this pair from enjoying a few drinks or a hearty meal. They decide to celebrate their new-found independence by visit-ing a steamy bar in the village. There, Ace appreciates—a little too obviously—Mima (Dorothy Lamour), the female half of the floor show. When her partner Caesar (Anthony Quinn), whose sadistic specialties include slinging Mima around the dance floor and removing cigarettes from her mouth with a whip, notices that Mima is responding positively to Lannigan's advances, he turns his whip on the two Americans.

Ace and Josh decide it's time to leave and escape through a window with Mima. The two enter into an innocent communal living arrangement with her, their bliss interrupted only by fear of Mima's growing domesticity, visits by Caesar, and hunger. By the time Josh's father and fiancée show up, both Josh and Ace are competing for Mima's hand. Frightened by the Mallon millions, she chooses Ace, and a dejected Josh leaves with his betrothed on his father's yacht. The problem is that one moonlit night Josh sang "I'm Too Romantic" to Mima and forever captured her heart. Ace, ecstatic at first, sees that she's not as happy as she ought to be and realizes what she's done ("Ah, so that's it. You went noble, huh?").

Things may seem bleak, but re-lax. In the "Road" series, there is no such thing as an unhappy ending. By a fortunate coincidence, the three are reunited and true love wins out.

Bing and Dorothy may have always sailed into the sunset in each other's arms, but Bob consistently walked away with the best notices for his performances in the "Road" pictures. *Singapore* was no exception. One reviewer called the road closed and blamed the dame in the sarong. Nor was Bing treated any more kindly. The *New York Times* critic wrote, "Mr. Crosby stares wistfully over the taffrail and croons his laryngeal best."

Singapore was the only "Road" picture to receive unfavorable reviews, although Lamour was never

ROAD TO SINGAPORE (1940). With Bob Hope and Allen Pomeroy

ROAD TO ZANZIBAR (1941). With Dorothy Lamour and Bob Hope

to be assessed in other than a cruel light. Ironically, the reviews of the six films that followed hailed the same wit and wackiness that the initial reviews deplored. Even Bing, seldom a favorite of critics in the "Road" pictures, began to receive some praise—albeit grudgingly at first.

The critics were unfair. *Singapore* is one of the best films in the series and, as the first, should have received credit for being remarkably innovative. Although there are moments that seem improvisatory, there is none of the excess of ad-libbing and spur-of-the-moment zaniness that diminishes some of the later films.

Dorothy Lamour's limitations as an actress have been overstated. Furthermore, if it doesn't seem too sexist to say it, she is so breathtaking in *Singapore* that it doesn't matter that she wears the same skirt and blouse throughout. When she tries on a pair of nylons that Josh has bought for her, she pulls them over her thighs with such natural sexiness that we find the scene blood-pulsing, despite its relative innocence.

We also find in *Singapore* many of the refreshing touches that were so successful with moviegoers that they became running gags. The famous "patty-cake" routine with which Crosby and Hope initiate every fight is a pleasant shock in *Singapore*; it is a familiar delight in the subsequent films.

Above all, *Road to Singapore* sets the wacky tone and dynamic pace and exhibits the sophisticated wit that distinguishes, to greater or lesser extent, the series. As a team, Crosby and Hope generate so much exuberant energy that it's not hard to understand their success. In "Captain Custard," one of *Singapore*'s song-and-dance duets, Hope sings, "We're in there pitchin' for Paramount." We believe him.

Despite the critic's sour prediction, the road was indeed not in danger of closing. *Road to Zanzibar* was released a year later and was an even bigger hit than *Singapore*. The Butler, Hartman, Schertzinger, and Burke team again went into action, with the added talent of composer Jimmy Van Heusen.

Zanzibar is not as tightly framed by its story as *Singapore*. The Hope and Crosby ad-libbing, however, is at its restrained best; we neither miss the structure nor mind the spontaneity. It's a footloose film that's funny—often hilarious, often ingenious.

This time around, Crosby is Chuck Reardon, carnival pro-

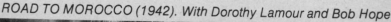

ROAD TO MOROCCO (1942). With Dorothy Lamour and Bob Hope

moter, and Hope is Hubert Frazier, his boyhood buddy and only act. Heading home from an African engagement, the boys invest their savings in a phony diamond mine, then retrieve the money by swindling someone else. Later they fall into the hands of two ruinous gold diggers; Donna Latour (Lamour) and Julia Quimby (Una Merkel). They con Chuck and Hubert into financing a safari so that Donna can "visit her sick father." Donna is actually heading for the nearest millionaire, a young man who rules a vast tea empire. Of course, this is before Donna has taken a moonlight ride on a jungle stream with the Crooner. Romance is temporarily thwarted when Chuck and Hubert fall into the hands of cannibals, but the boys escape via their "patty-cake" routine, and Chuck and Donna get back together for a closing embrace.

In *Zanzibar*, Hope and Crosby establish their "Road" personas. *Singapore* portrays them more or less as equals; in this movie, Hope begins to emerge as a wide-eyed, pathetic "schlump." He is the victim of Bing's sly schemes, the lovesick loser in the contest over Dorothy, the brunt of every irony. Bing becomes a sympathetic comedian, the straight man to Hope's dope. More than anything else, Bob's rubbery-faced anxiety, pitted against Bing's unflappable surface, made the pure fun that won the fans. This genre of comedic pairing is commonplace. It had worked before them with Laurel and Hardy and would work later with Martin and Lewis. But Hope and Crosby were different. They had an inherent sophistication and a featherlight touch that make them, even today, the masters of this particular style of humor.

By the time we get to *Morocco* in 1942, Hope and Crosby substitute so much of their own ad-libbing in place of the script that the film seems a little out of control. Since it's the same Butler-Hartman-Burke-Van Heusen team that was responsible for *Singapore* and *Zanzibar*, we can find only two possible sources upon which to lay the blame: the change in directors from Victor Schertzinger to David Butler (no relation to Frank), or overconfidence due to the success of the series.

At any rate, *Morocco* falls flat—despite the catchy "Road to Morocco" theme song, which has made it the best-known of the films. There are too many self-conscious asides to the audience, too many reprises of unsuccessful gags used in the previous pictures, too much of an unrehearsed, free-form quality, and far too much slaphappy wackiness. When their "patty-cake" routine doesn't work, Hope says to Crosby, "That thing sure got around." A camel remarks casually to the audience, "This is the screw-

ROAD TO MOROCCO (1942). With Dorothy Lamour

ROAD TO UTOPIA (1946). With Dorothy Lamour and Bob Hope

iest picture I was ever in." After being tied up and left in the desert to die, Bing and Bob mysteriously get free and tell us that if they revealed how they did it, we'd never believe them. We're warned in the beginning that they'll probably run into Dorothy Lamour and that they're sure to get into trouble, but "Paramount will protect us 'cause we're signed for five more years."

Road to Morocco is undisciplined slapstick with Bing and Bob throwing "insults instead of custard pies." Still, there are inspired moments. As the two are stumbling their way through the desert, they see a mirage of Dorothy Lamour emerging from the sand. "She must have been visiting a gopher friend," says Bob. There's a zany free-for-all with Anthony Quinn (who is back this time as Sheik Mullay Kasim) in his tent, a nodding-head sequence in the palace of Princess Shalmar (Lamour) that is side-splitting, and romance personified in Bing's rendition of "Moonlight Becomes You."

In early 1946, the fourth "Road" film, *Road to Utopia*, was released. It had been made in late 1944 but was not introduced until

ROAD TO UTOPIA (1946). With Dorothy Lamour and Bob Hope

1946, perhaps because of the continuing success of the pious *Going My Way* and *The Bells of St. Mary's*. The location was not Utopia but Skagway, Alaska, during the Gold Rush days. In fact, the location—with its mining-camp desolation and artificial blizzards—may have been chosen as a flattering imitation of Chaplin's popular *The Gold Rush* (re-released in 1942 with a soundtrack).

Two of Hope's former radio writers, Norman Panama and Melvin Frank, replaced screenwriters Butler and Hartman (who was later to become head of Paramount). The studio also brought in a new director, Hal Walker, but retained the songwriting services of Van Heusen and Burke.

Road to Utopia is the favorite of a number of "Road" film fanatics. The picture does maintain a high pitch of amiable lunacy, but this time the wackiness has direction. It is here that Crosby and Hope reach their summit as a comedy team. As Bosley Crowther wrote in his *New York Times* review of the movie, "Their style seems more refined, their timing a little more expert, their insults a little more acute."

The script is amazingly similar to that of *Zanzibar*. Bing and Bob—this time a pair of vaudeville confidence men—find themselves once more in a remote region. Bob, ever homesick, wants to go back to New York, but Bing, the soldier of fortune, ties up their finances in another get-rich-quick scheme, this one involving a secret map to a gold mine. In the typically convoluted manner of the "Road" films, when they finally arrive at the mine, they discover it belongs to none other than Miss Lamour. Of course, there are songs, dances, and an endless series of miraculous escapes.

Bing and Bob encountered real hazards in making *Utopia*. The day after shooting a sequence with a live bear, it went berserk and tore off its trainer's arm. One scene had them walking tenuously on the side of a fake glacier with an authentic fifty-foot drop on both sides. A rope broke as they were climbing a mountain in another scene and Bing fell on top of Bob and injured his back. "In those days," says Hope, "we were numbers one and two at the box office. Paramount didn't care—I guess it was another way of dropping your option."

Road to Utopia is a nearly perfect comedy—fast-paced and different. The dialogue is surprisingly risqué for the period, but its tone is worldly rather than cheap. The most winning feature of *Utopia* is Robert Benchley who, occasionally and inexplicably, interrupts the action to give a bizarre explanation of filmmaking techniques.

ROAD TO RIO (1948). With Bob Hope and Dorothy Lamour

For *Road to Rio*, released in 1948, Crosby and Hope each took a one-third partnership (with Paramount holding the remaining third) in the financing of the film. Although Bing was not able to raise his share of the needed money from California bankers and had to turn to New York, this was one investment that was no gamble. *Rio* turned out to be as lucrative as the other cities the pair had visited.

The story and screenplay were by Edmund Beloin and Jack Rose, with Norman Z. McLeod directing. Johnny Burke and Jimmy Van Heusen were still writing the music; however, this is the first time the choreography—by Bernard Pearce and Billy Daniels—was given serious attention.

The "Road" films usually had at least one elaborately staged—and often quite intriguing—musical number with a myriad of singers, dancers, and extras in native costume. (In *Singapore* and *Zanzibar* the major dance sequences are especially noteworthy.) *Road to Rio*, however, surpasses them all musically. Not only does it present Bing crooning with Bob and to Dorothy, it also presents the talents of the Andrews Sisters, the Wiere Brothers, the Carioca Boys, the Stone-Barton Puppeteers, and what seems like the entire population of Rio happily swinging its hips to the samba beat.

The music appears at the expense of the comedy, which is not as consistently sharp as in the other pictures. Still, there are—as always—those uproarious moments that make even the worst "Road" pictures worth seeing. It's good to see Jerry Colonna (who gives a priceless performance as Achilles Bombanassa in *Road to Singapore*) once again. Colonna is as memorable a cavalry captain as he was the eccentric resident of Kaigoon.

Scat Sweeney (Bing) and Hot Lips Barton (Bob), two itinerant musicians, wander into the same kinds of trouble they've been in before at the hands of Lamour (here a stunning señorita). Hope is funniest when, as a stowaway, he finds himself being hung up as a ham in the ship's refrigerator. It's Bing, however, who's in peak form here. *The New York Times* called him "the smoothest straight man in the business today . . . feeding jokes to his pal when he doesn't actually steal the play by adding a snapper to a snapper."

Five years elapsed before Bing, Bob, and Dorothy again took to the road. In 1953, Paramount released

ROAD TO BALI (1953). With Dorothy Lamour and Bob Hope

Road to Bali, again produced in partnership with its two stars—except that this time Bing Crosby Enterprises and Bob Hope Enterprises held the copyrights. It was the first "Road" film to be photographed in color and received much publicity from its $1,000,000 budget, a good deal of which was spent in experimental photography. One of the best "studio executive" stories emerged from the making of *Bali*. Adolph Zukor, then president of Paramount, cut from the finished print an underwater ballet sequence that had cost a great deal because of its ingeniously utilized trick photography. Why? "Because it was so boring."

With or without the water ballet, *Bali* looks like a million. The set captures everyone's ideal of a tropical isle, with scanty sarongs on beautiful girls, birds barely hidden in flower-laden bushes, and color, color, color.

In this go-round, the boys—to no surprise a pair of vaudevillians—encounter their familiar nemesis in the person of Princess Lalah. They search for sunken treasure and save both the loot and the lady from the clutches of a wicked prince.

Hal Walker, whose instincts for slightly toning down the Crosby-Hope exuberance made *Road to Utopia* one of the best films in the series, directed here with the same results. However, the services of the Burke-Van Heusen team are conspicuously absent. *Bali* is as musically barren as *Rio* was rich. Even Bing is unable to save the sparse and indifferent score. We are inclined to agree with Bob when, seeing that his friend is about to sing, he tells the audience, "Now's the time to go out and get the popcorn." Except for its music, *Bali* looks like it was good for our three stars. They seem so genuinely happy to be reunited that we can't help cavorting along with them.

In addition to the standard Hope-Crosby banter—which is at a high level of comedic professionalism here—*Bali* serves up more than the usual number of unorthodox touches. In this marvelous land, gorillas—not monkeys—swing from vines, and a giant squid watches over the submerged treasure. In brief uncredited appearances, Humphrey Bogart, Jane Russell, Dean Martin, and Jerry Lewis make adroit use of the cameo device. A clip from *The African Queen*, showing Bogart dragging his boat through the jungle swamp, was cut into the action, and Jane Russell dances cobra-style from a magic basket. Surprisingly, the best of the guest spots comes from Bing's brother, Bob. He steps out from the tropical undergrowth, coolly fires a rifle, and tells the audience that his brother promised him "one shot" in the film.

ROAD TO BALI (1953). With Bob Hope

ROAD TO HONG KONG (1962). With Bob Hope

Perhaps Bing had to make a small sacrifice to bring Bob Crosby into the picture: *Bali* is the only one of the seven "Road" films in which Hope gets top billing.

When we find Bing, Bob, and Dorothy reunited for the last time in 1962, it is sad to see them growing older but good to see them together again. *Hong Kong* detours from the traditional road in a number of important respects. Filmed at England's Shepperton Studios in less than four months, it is the first "Road" movie to be made outside of Hollywood. It is also the only picture in the series that was not made under the aegis of Paramount. *Road to Hong Kong* is a United Artists release—but written, directed, and produced by

the same Panama-Frank team that wrote the screenplay for *Road to Utopia*. And, regrettably, a middle-aged and somewhat matronly Dorothy Lamour was no longer able to play "the sexy sarong girl." In response to Hope's fervent pleas, however, she consented to make a brief appearance for old time's sake. Her stock part went to Joan Collins, who, inexplicably, was chosen over such tough competition as Brigitte Bardot, Gina Lollobrigida, and Sophia Loren.

"Road" fans didn't seem to mind the alterations. *Hong Kong* was the fifth most successful film in 1962. Crosby and Hope each bore a third of the picture's financing—this time in partnership with Melvin Frank and Norman Panama instead of

ROAD TO HONG KONG (1962). As Harry Turner

with Paramount. Each star—already fabulously wealthy—picked up an additional $2,000,000 from the box office in return for his investment.

It's ironic that *Road to Hong Kong* seems dated today, when some of the "Road" pictures made two decades before have not begun to wear out their welcome. Despite the success, the film's merits lie more in its sentimental journeying than in its comedy.

Hong Kong has a number of distinguished guest stars, among them Robert Morley, David Niven, and Frank Sinatra. A brilliant performance by Peter Sellers as an East Indian doctor is, in itself, worth the price of admission. And it seems that Hope and Crosby simply cannot get in each other's company and not make us laugh. It's just that what once seemed brisk has slowed down with age, what once seemed innovative has become stale, and the sophistication of the Bing-Bob brand of craziness often crosses the thin line into corn. Further, Bing is no longer a credible heartthrob. As even he admitted at the time, he was "too old to get the girl and not old enough to be her granddad." Finally, the glorious escapism of the "Road" essence is lost in the mundane scientism of a space-age farce. Its intrigue, its rockets, its espionage rings make *Road to Hong Kong* a little too modern to be as much fun as the others.

The Crosby-Hope competitiveness—on and off the road—has become famous. According to Dorothy Lamour, "You kind of had the feeling that maybe they stayed home the night before and read their scripts to see who could outdo the other." In reality, they became such good friends that the Hope and Crosby families lived together in the same twenty-two bedroom English manor house throughout the filming of *Road to Hong Kong*. Despite the wisecracking which still continues, they remain almost Siamese buddies. Bob Hope summed up their relationship when he commented recently, "Nobody has ever reached [Bing's] proportions, and I hope he never reads this because I don't want him to think that I care for him."

The "Road" series became so warmly familiar that during World War II troops overseas were cheered by *Road to Victory*, a one-reel propaganda film with Bing Crosby singing the title song. Hope and Crosby were the original "dynamic duo." As Bosley Crowther put it, "Apart, they may be very funny or clever or quaint or what you will, according to where you are sitting and what sort of picture they're in. But together, and in a 'Road' picture, with the consequent freedom of style and reckless impulse that goes with it, they are pretty nigh nonpareil."

The focus of Bing Crosby's film career changed in the mid-forties with his memorable portrayal of Father O'Malley in *Going My Way*. Perhaps because he was encouraged by the favorable response of both general audiences and critics to a role that was less frivolous than dramatic, perhaps because he was growing less credible as a romantic lead with the passing years, perhaps simply because he wanted to try something new, Bing's latter films are increasingly sober. Surprisingly, the transition may have been more difficult for Bing's audiences than for Bing. Once we accept him as a serious actor, we see that he is as deft in drama as in other lighter genres. His instinctive naturalness adds to the realism, his tendency to under- rather than overplay adds subtlety, his matured character adds strength.

Strangely enough, an early film, *Sing You Sinners* (1938), foreshadows the breadth of Bing's range. Although it was called "the funniest comedy on Broadway, including all the side streets," from a modern vantage point it is comedic only in the blackest sense and even then it has a grim underside. Only if one is inclined to laugh heartily at *The Grapes of Wrath* will he be amused by this downbeat movie about the Depression struggles of a family that is crippled by one member who refuses to carry his

MEN OF THE CLOTH ... AND THE BOTTLE

own weight. Considering the ragged clothes, the frayed and dusty quality of life that, even though photographed in black and white, cakes everything with an odd sepia hue, the wretched search for a dollar that puts loving family members at each other's throats—*Sing You Sinners*, despite its comedy and music, offers little in the way of merriment.

The story, by Claude Binyon, centers around the bleak poverty and unrealized dreams of "Maw" Beebe (Elizabeth Patterson), a widow, and her three sons: indolent Joe (Bing Crosby), steadfast David (Fred MacMurray), and precocious little Mike (Donald O'Connor). Wesley Ruggles directed with his hand firmly on the audience's heartstrings, and the result is too lugubrious for even Bing to lighten. Still, Crosby diminishes the melodrama by his touching performance as the irresponsible millstone around his family's neck. We, like they, desperately wish for his reform.

The genial ne'er-do-well is Bing Crosby's screen persona. Even in his most feathery musical comedies, he tends to be a drifter and dreamer. Although we often glimpse the dark overtones of this wayward spirit, here the dangerous-

SING YOU SINNERS (1938). On the set with
director Wesley Ruggles and Donald O'Connor

ly self-indulgent wastrel emerges full face. Although in retrospect Bing's performance seems under-developed and immature, Joe Beebe anticipates the self-pitying alcoholic of *The Country Girl*, the betrayed and embittered husband of *Man on Fire*, and the emotion-ally withdrawn father of *Little Boy Lost*. The pinnacle of *Sing You Sinners* is a scene in which Joe ruins a family dinner celebrating his new job by revealing that he lost it the first day. He calmly continues to eat as everyone leaves the dining room one by one in tears. Finally,

alone at the family's massive table, Joe realizes how much he has dis-appointed his family and loses his appetite. He sits disconsolately con-fronting his failure.

Sing You Sinners was regarded by the critics of 1938 as a water-shed in Bing Crosby's career. They applauded the film's comedy, the song "Small Fry" by Frank Loesser and Hoagy Carmichael, and the "lovable" performance of Bing Crosby. It could be that the period was so bleak and that Americans were by then so inured to hardship that they were indiffer-

SING YOU SINNERS (1938). With Fred MacMurray, Ellen Drew, Elizabeth Patterson, and Donald O'Connor

ent to the film's dispiriting soup kitchen and bread line atmosphere. Money—searching for it, losing it, scrounging along without it—is the center of the story and the source of any humor which emerges. Life has music for the Beebes only because the three brothers must sing for their supper. And there's something irredeemably pathetic about seeing a "small fry" so heavily burdened by his family's problems.

Joe says to David, "You're America's big brother. Honest, hard-working and stupid as a duck." "Maw" Beebe says to Joe, "Well, where do we go from here, Big Shot?" And everyone says to everyone else, "You're gonna pay me, ain't ya?" These lines capture the melancholy viewpoint of *Sing You Sinners*, a film in which Bing sounded new depths.

If *Sing You Sinners* was a signpost, *Going My Way* was the destination. The highly acclaimed film about the changing of the guard from old to new in a metropolitan parish is the most important film in Bing Crosby's career. It provided a rich vehicle in which to discover and polish previously unappreciated facets of his talent; it established him with both the public

GOING MY WAY (1944). With Barry Fitzgerald

and the critics as a capable dramatic actor; it created an entirely new and antithetical screen image—one which still haunts him. It also resulted in an important addition to his trophy chest, the Academy Award for the Best Actor of 1944. After his fine performance as Father O'Malley, the progressive parish priest, Bing received the highest of accolades: he was taken seriously.

Ironically, Crosby turned down the O'Malley role when producer-director Leo McCarey first offered it to him. Initially, McCarey had only conceived a vague story for a movie about the priesthood to be called *The Padre*, but he felt intuitively that his good friend Crosby was perfect for the lead. Bing was convinced that "the Church simply wouldn't stand for that kind of casting." He was comfortable playing a high-living scapegrace because the role was similar to his own lifestyle. But he had never been too priestly. Still, he had always wanted to work with McCarey, felt flattered and challenged, and finally let himself be persuaded to slip into the stiff white collar.

McCarey was so deeply com-

GOING MY WAY (1944). With Gene Lockhart

mitted to his idea that he invested his entire life savings in developing the project. First, he fought to sign Bing. His second happy decision was the casting of the Irish actor Barry Fitzgerald as the crotchety counterpart to Crosby's O'Malley. The one rainy evening he stopped to pick up a hitchhiking sailor. The sailor looked in the car as McCarey pulled up and said, "Going my way?" The project suddenly had a new title, and McCarey's way proved once more to be the right direction.

Frank Butler and Frank Cavett turned the original idea into a screenplay, but McCarey was always willing to modify the shooting script if he felt his stars could add something on their own or if he was convinced that a brainstorm he'd had the night before would work more effectively. The loose and informal structure resulted in many of the unexpected, gem-like touches that brighten the film. According to mezzo-soprano Risë Stevens, Bing's co-star, the film's greatest asset—its warmth—was the genuine product of the natural rapport which grew up between Crosby and Fitzgerald in the fertile soil of McCarey's direction.

Going My Way is the story of a vibrant and innovative young curate (Crosby) who has been sent to rescue a poor urban parish from the financial and moral decay which has set in over the years. His mission is to quietly take over the administration of the parish, gently nudging aside the conservative and enfeebled pastor (Fitzgerald). The old man has literally built the parish with his own hands and now stands trusting in God to bring better days again. A touching bond develops between the two men, as each works in his own way to save the parish.

It is a charming tale which is written, acted, and directed with simple dignity. Bing patterned Father O'Malley on a priest who had greatly influenced him during his days at Gonzaga. Father Fitzgibbon had a prototype too—an eccentric priest in Palm Springs. But the feisty and endearing little Fitzgerald forever claimed the character as his own.

There is also good music—much of it by Johnny Burke and Jimmy Van Heusen. The members of the Robert Mitchell Boy Choir are dressed as street urchins, but they sing and look more like Botticelli's angels than gamins. Bing sings "Silent Night," and his subsequent recording nearly matched "White Christmas" in record sales. The film even finds time for Risë Stevens to sing the "Habañera" from *Carmen* (her most famous role); the sequence is cleverly integrated into the story. Back on the pop level, a new song by Burke and Van Heusen, "Swinging on a Star," won an Oscar for Best Song.

GOING MY WAY (1944). With Barry Fitzgerald and Risë Stevens

Not only did it win the Oscar for Best Song—*Going My Way* walked off with most of the honors at the 1944 Academy Award ceremonies. Barry Fitzgerald was named Best Supporting Actor; Leo McCarey, Best Director; and Butler and Cavett won the award for Best Screenplay. Bing, who was honored by the nomination for Best Actor but didn't dream he had a chance of winning, was playing golf only a short time before the ceremonies. Friends convinced him to put down his clubs and attend. The moment when his pal, Gary Cooper, announced his name was one of the few in Bing's life when his breezy composure slipped decisively.

There were other rewards as well. The movie earned more than $7 million for Paramount and—irony of ironies—Pope Pius XII wrote Bing a letter to tell him how much he enjoyed seeing the priesthood "humanized."

Bing's identification with the clergy became so strong after *Going My Way* that he was avalanched by requests for spiritual advice. One critic wrote, "After all the times Bing Crosby has played a priest in films, you'd think by now he would be a Bishop or a Mon-

THE BELLS OF ST. MARY'S (1945). With Ingrid Bergman

THE BELLS OF ST. MARY'S (1945). With Ingrid Bergman and the parish children

signor, at least." Actually, Bing would don a cassock only three times in his entire screen career. It just seemed as if he had always played priests.

Audiences didn't seem to mind that the two other movies in which Bing became Father Crosby were artistically disappointing. The public flocked to both *The Bells of St. Mary's* (1945) and *Say One for Me* (1959). Encouraged by his success with *Going My Way*, McCarey immediately set to work on a sequel, *The Bells of St. Mary's*, which answered the question of where Father O'Malley went when he walked off into the night at the end of *Going My Way*. He went, it seems, to help a troubled Catholic school headed by an idealistic Mother Superior (Ingrid Bergman). As usual, he puts everything into working order again with a casual but effective touch.

Thankfully, Bing is pretty nearly the same Chuck O'Malley. Everything else, unfortunately, is also the same. McCarey was trying too hard to squeeze his film into a pre-existing mold. He makes too obvious an attempt to find new situations that will duplicate the old clerical charm, too little an attempt to create a new movie. The carbon copy is formulaic and uninteresting. The spontaneity is gone. As Sister Benedict, Ingrid Bergman is a little too noble, a little too

saccharine; she's missing the raw, irascible side that made Father Fitzgibbon both appealing and believable. In a scene where she gives boxing lessons to a boy who will not stand up for himself, we can't help sighing at the exaggeration inherent in a nun with her dukes up.

The Bells of St. Mary's is an adequate film, occasionally poignant but never deeply engrossing. We are happy to see the recurrent hint of romance between O'Malley and Benedict—it is a sign of vulnerability, like Fitzgibbon's occasional nip of Old Bushmills, that makes it all less beatific, a little closer to earth than heaven.

Say One for Me (1959) was 20th Century-Fox's attempt to cash in on Crosby as cleric. However, the studio was unwilling to prop up an entire film on its aging star's devout image; instead, he is given a parish near Broadway and thrust into the show-biz milieu that marked his early crooning days. The result is a film with fewer dramatic pretensions and yet less diversion than any of its predecessors in Crosby's serious work. The transition in Bing's career is symbolized by the fact that he is not one of the movie's troupers, as he would have been in the old days; he is the priest who enters troubled lives and affects them in meaningful ways. His Father Conroy is Chuck O'Malley grown fifteen years older.

Although Bing could not, of

SAY ONE FOR ME (1959). With Debbie Reynolds and Les Tremayne

course, be at once priest and romantic lead, we resent Robert Wagner as the impious nightclub headliner that Bing used to be. Wagner marries the showgirl (Debbie Reynolds) and Bing just performs the ceremony. Crosby croons a few tunes and saves alcoholics and unwed mothers—in this case with an excess of calm. The film makes us nostalgic for the days before he took his vows.

Say One for Me is pleasant, if undistinguished, entertainment. Robert O'Brien's screenplay and Frank Tashlin's direction look more toward Broadway than toward Rome. Father Conroy good-naturedly adjusts his post to his clientele—he calls his 2:00 A.M. mass the "late, late, *late* show." After seeing *Say One for Me*, a contemporary said that he finally understood why Bing had been so startlingly successful in portraying priests. He was the embodiment of what we wanted from our own organized religions. The garb provided the piety; Bing provided the humanity. As the man put it, when he turns down his collar, we expect to see a sports shirt underneath.

It was as inevitable that Bing would be reunited with Barry Fitzgerald as that he would return to the cloth. Crosby and Fitzgerald appeared together two more times: in 1947, for *Welcome Stranger*, a remake of *Going My Way*, with Bing brandishing a stethoscope instead of a rosary; and *Top o' the Morning* (1949), an offhanded bit of whimsy co-starring Ann Blyth that was, not too surprisingly, set in Ireland.

Fans of *Going My Way* rushed to see *Welcome Stranger*, and few of them were disappointed. The film compares more favorably with its model than *The Bells of St.* *Mary's*. A comedy-drama about a conservative, elderly doctor who feels threatened by his upstart young "assistant," *Welcome Stranger* succeeds in putting a lump in our throats. We've seen a reluctant bond grow between these two men before, but it's got a certain residual magic. Despite all our efforts at cynicism, our emotions succumb to such gimmicks as a climactic scene in which Crosby must save the life of his grizzled superior with an emergency appendectomy.

Unlike *Going My Way*, with its fresh, imaginative touches, *Welcome Stranger* owes less to its

WELCOME STRANGER (1947). With Joan Caulfield and Barry Fitzgerald

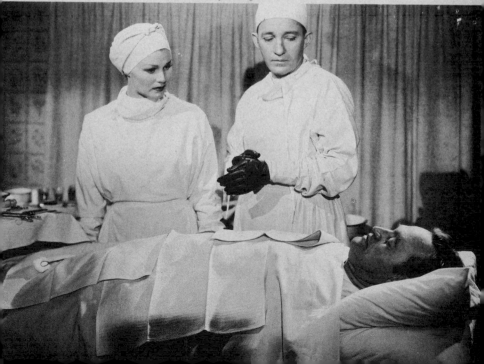

script than to the star quality of its two leads. Fitzgerald's flinty little Irishman is the perfect complement to Crosby's young doctor, and together they are remarkably successful at filling up the screen. In Fitzgerald's hands, Doc McRory becomes almost as colorful a character as Father Fitzgibbon. Bing, however, is faced with adding flesh to the rather skeletal character of the youthful Dr. Pearson. He is excellent. We sense vulnerability under the flashy and self-confident surface and want him to find acceptance among the clannish New England townspeople and their vinegary physician. Since doctors are not required to make vows of celibacy, romance can flower in Pearson's life. The young woman who captures his heart is the vapid Joan Caulfield, who, as usual, adds nothing but her beauty.

The premise of *Top o' the Morning* is the theft of the Blarney Stone, and the story includes an American insurance investigator (Crosby) who—inexplicably—is sent to Ireland to solve the mystery; an irresistible old curmudgeon of a policeman (Fitzgerald); his winsome and toothsome daughter (Blyth); and a ruck of local characters with brogues as thick as Irish stew. No doubt intended as a

TOP O' THE MORNING (1949). With Ann Blyth

JUST FOR YOU (1952). With Jane Wyman

*LITTLE BOY LOST (1953). With Christian Fourcade
and Gabrielle Dorziat*

LITTLE BOY LOST (1953). With Christian Fourcade

THE COUNTRY GIRL (1954). With Grace Kelly

little bit of heaven that nestled on the Paramount lot, *Top o' the Morning* lands with a distinct thud. Its quaint old airs and twinkly-eyed, upturned humor seem pretty forced. It's only redeeming feature is Bing's rendition of "When Irish Eyes Are Smiling."

The last of Bing's comedy dramas started a new trend—Bing as father. *Just for You*, released in 1952, capitalized on the popular *Here Comes the Groom* (1951). Bing starred with Jane Wyman in both vehicles, but the similarities between the two end there. Graying and solemn, he plays a widower and father of two children who is torn between a burgeoning romance

with Miss Wyman and the pressures of raising a difficult eighteen-year-old son who also has a puerile eye on his pop's lady. Bing finally ends up with Miss Wyman and the son ends up a man—although the credit must go to the armed forces rather than his father.

Drably directed by Elliott Nugent, *Just for You* is a tiring and lackluster effort. The screenplay by Robert Carson, based on Stephen Vincent Benet's story "Famous," would be better without its occasional dramatic pretensions. Robert Arthur's asinine portrayal of the son further emphasizes the script's inherent unreality. He is supposed to be eighteen, not eight.

THE COUNTRY GIRL (1954). With William Holden

There is also music—an occasional vaporous, insignificant song that interrupts the family squabbling and is forgotten the instant it ends. The only graceful moments occur when the lovely Ms. Wyman appears.

Just for You, however, has one note of distinction in the performance of Ethel Barrymore as the headmistress of a finishing school to which Bing would like to send his daughter (Natalie Wood). Bing is so lifeless and unfocused in this one that we can only assume he is embarrassed by the whole film.

Although Bing has always considered himself a crooner instead of an actor, *Little Boy Lost* proved him wrong. Until 1953, when this quiet and deeply emotional film was released, Crosby—even at his most dramatic—was considered (and considered himself) a lightweight. *Little Boy Lost* marks the second turning point of Bing's film career. The startling evolution of his craft over the years and the depth of his talent are apparent in this film for the first time. It was followed by what might be termed the mature phase of his development and is distinguished by serious dramatic achievement.

Little Boy Lost is the story of a man's attempt to find his lost son. By means of flashbacks, we learn that Bill Wainwright (Crosby) is an American journalist who was working in France during World War II. His French wife was killed by the Nazis and his infant son disappeared. As the film opens, he is returning to France in hopes of finding his child. A lead he has uncovered takes him to a Catholic orphanage outside Paris, where he finds a boy (Christian Fourçade) whose background is similar to his son's. The two revisit places which the boy might find familiar, thus verifying his identity. It is a tortuous journey that reveals a man tied morbidly to his memories. It is not the son but the wife that he wants to find again. It is not the little boy but the father who is lost.

The greatest credit for *Little Boy Lost* should go to director George Seaton. Seaton was so taken with the Marghanita Laski story on which the film is based that he himself adapted it for the screen. He is also responsible for the casting of Bing as the American father, a decision which was thought highly questionable. Both author Laski and Paramount executives insisted that American audiences and critics would not find the crooner credible in a film that offered little music and absolutely no humor. The Cassandras changed their minds after seeing Bing's outstanding performance.

Crosby's life had its own share of tragedy at the time, which may have helped his performance. Dixie Lee, his wife of twenty-two years, was stricken with cancer and died during the making of the film. Bing

THE COUNTRY GIRL (1954). With William Holden

received the news that she was dying moments before the shooting of a scene in which he was to walk to the station to catch the train back to Paris, convinced that the child he had just seen in the orphanage was not his. Seaton recalls the scene, one of the most touching of the film: "I remember the way he carried that suitcase. He had the whole weight of the world on his shoulders. When he got to the platform, I yelled 'Cut' and looked around to find half the crew was crying."

Filmed in France, *Little Boy Lost* has a European flavor, almost as if it were an arthouse import. Fourçade imprints his wide, sorrowful eyes and spindly, tubercular frame forever into our hearts. A scene in which the American gives the boy his first present—a pair of gloves that are too small—is wrenching without being overdone. Seaton has put together a profoundly touching statement of the effects of war and, on a more personal level, of love. The genuine tragedy of the story stays with us long after the film has ended.

The next property that attracted

Seaton resulted in Bing's most highly acclaimed role—that of Frank Elgin in Clifford Odets' *The Country Girl* (1954). Seaton adapted Odets' play for the screen —once more proving his uncompromising commitment to an original work and its author's unique style and vision.

There are some changes in Odets' text, however, Seaton turned Elgin into a musical star and added songs by Harold Arlen and Ira Gershwin, but he did not sacrifice the playwright's hard-hitting plot or the crisp, colloquial poetry of his dialogue.

The Country Girl probes the innermost motivations and frailties of its three principal characters: an alcoholic actor, his long-suffering wife, and an arrogant stage director. It is, in the apt words of one critic, a "searching and pitiless thing"—a brutal examination of shame, self-destructiveness, and fortitude. And yet there is a thin veneer of optimism: man has finer instincts; his eyes are sometimes on the stars.

Again, as with *Little Boy Lost*, problems resulted when Seaton insisted upon following his unorthodox preferences for casting. Seaton had added the musical touches —however minor—because he

MAN ON FIRE (1957). With Mary Fickett

MAN ON FIRE (1957). With (left to right) Anne Seymour, Richard Eastham, Mary Fickett, Inger Stevens, Malcolm Brodrick, and E.G. Marshall

wanted Bing Crosby in the principal role. This time the strongest objections came from Bing. It was unlike anything he had ever attempted. The complexities of Elgin's neuroses left too much room for failure. Even after he had signed to do the role, his acquiescence remained shaky and reluctant.

As if his headaches weren't severe enough already, Seaton chose Grace Kelly to play the worn and humiliated wife. Kelly had very much wanted the part and felt she could handle it. Still, up to then her career had been limited to elegant fashion magazine beauties, cool and classy. Although Georgie Elgin was indelibly wearing the remnants of a proud and cultured past, she had definitely seen better days.

Seaton completed the triumvirate of stars with William Holden as Bernie Dodd. Although Holden was certainly a safer bet than Kelly or Crosby, he also provided his share of risk. As the tough but tender director who misguidedly struggles for Elgin's comeback by attacking the singer's wife, Holden would have to evince enough hardboiled creative force and Times Square smarts to make the audience believe he could direct Broadway plays.

The first few days of shooting were beset by such nervous strain that even Seaton's iron conviction in the rightness of his decision began to falter. Finally, he scrapped everything that had been shot up to that point and began anew. The stars finally lost their self-consciousness and submitted to Seaton's strong directorial hand. The project was completed in little more than five weeks.

Grace Kelly's Georgie Elgin won her that year's Academy Award for Best Actress. Bing received an Oscar nomination for Best Actor but lost to Marlon Brando for his performance in *On the Waterfront*. After the nominations were announced, Hollywood became bitterly divided into Crosby and Brando camps.

Despite his reputation for insouciance, Bing was anything but casual about acting Frank Elgin. His is a trenchant and moving performance, as honest as Paul Kelly's much-heralded stage version. Crosby gives this dissipated loser a pathetic humility that disguises the brutality of his real selfishness. His quiet self-apologist is far more subtly drawn than the calculated rage of his stage counterpart.

Bing took his role so seriously that he did not sleep the night before a scene in which Elgin was to be in a Boston jail after an all-night binge. A regular sleeper, used to going to bed early, he enlisted the aid of his sons to stay up with him. They walked him arm-in-arm around their home each time he started to nod off. The result was so authentic that even his mother thought he'd been carousing. She showed up unexpectedly at the set and was horrified at the sight of her wobbly, bleary-eyed, and unshaven son. "Harry!," she scolded, and walked out in a huff.

Whether consciously or not, Bing had never allowed himself to be so degraded on the screen as in *The Country Girl*. His characters may have suffered from unrequited love or been victimized by their own negligent behavior or immature dreams, but he never relinquished the essential Crosby dignity. During most of *The Country Girl*, however, Frank Elgin remains steadfastly seedy; his alcoholism is proof against any nobler stature. Bing plunges willingly to the bottom of Elgin's humiliating weaknesses.

Man on Fire, made in 1957, is devastating drama—one of the most realistic studies of divorce ever made in Hollywood. It was Bing's last starring role as a serious actor and the only totally non-musical film of his career.

There are no heroes in *Man on*

STAGECOACH (1966). As Doc Boone

Fire. The central character is Earl Carleton (Crosby), a prosperous divorcé who finds himself embroiled in a bitter fight with his ex-wife (Mary Fickett) over the custody of their son Ted (Malcolm Brodrick). In court, a woman judge awards the boy to his mother—now remarried to Bryan Seward (Richard Eastham)—despite Ted's passionate devotion to Carleton. After a drinking bout, Carleton attempts to kidnap his son, who is deeply resistant to his mother's efforts at winning him over. The two are apprehended in an ugly scene at the airport, but, subsequently, Mrs. Seward decides to surrender any claim to Ted. Carleton is brought to his senses by her magnanimity and counters with a more equitable plan and a show of friendly conciliation.

The interesting twist to this commonplace plot is that both parents are reasonable, intelligent beings. The frailties which they occasionally exhibit in front of the boy—angry outbursts, humiliating tactics, irrational partisanship —are understandably human displays of emotional intensity. They have botched up their life together. Their son, a symbol of their failure, becomes the brunt of their frustrated bickerings. No longer in love with each other, they turn their love toward him. That love becomes perverted, its object scarred by the unconscious venality of their contest.

In the words of one critic, writer-director Ranald MacDougall created his screenplay "with the intelligence of a sociologist." His direction exhibits such control that, despite the emotionalism of the story, it never becomes overheated. Bing, especially, gives a moving and reasoned performance as Earl Carleton, the divorced father. He manages to portray Carleton's bouts of morbid self-pity without undue theatrics. He brings to the surface the man's complex motivations without spelling them out.

The power of this disturbing film lies in its realism, in its lack of manipulation or melodrama. It is a strong sermon against divorce; however, it is not through the film's proselytizing but rather through its thought-provoking examination of a problem that it establishes its worth. Bing's strong feelings against divorce gave him a deep commitment to the project; yet his performance is free of self-righteousness or pietism. The other actors—Inger Stevens as a possible new love in Bing's life, Lee J. Cobb as Bing's lawyer, Fickett and Eastham as the Sewards, Brodrick as the little boy—are encouraged to portray human beings rather than "types."

Despite the rumors that he has been, alternately, a severe and indifferent father in real life, Bing

STAGECOACH (1966). With Red Buttons

"plays" fathers with consummate sensitivity. These are roles which, like his priests, are highly ironic in view of his offscreen behavior.

Bing's last screen role to date was that of the drunken doctor in the 20th Century-Fox remake of John Ford's Western, *Stagecoach*. Released in 1966, the film gives Bing third billing under Ann-Margret and Michael Connors. It is one of the few Crosby pictures—including star-studded vehicles—in which he did not receive top billing.

The new *Stagecoach* was budgeted at $5 million and was able to utilize the visual benefits of CinemaScope; still, the film does not touch the shoulders of Ford's classic. Although Ford strongly disapproved of the idea of a remake, director Gordon Douglas was modest enough not to try to upstage his predecessor. Screenwriter Joseph Landon did not tamper seriously with Dudley Nichols' original script. The most drastic adjustment was a change in setting from the Arizona desert to the spectacular scenery of the Rocky Mountains so that new developments in photographic technique could be more fully utilized. Still, the casting was pitiful and wrecked the filmmakers' best efforts. Despite the fact that *Stagecoach* is a "horse opera" whose stereotyped characters act out predictable situations while taking a back seat to Indian raids, the all-star cast of minor talents was not up to even the limited demands made on them.

Only Bing (along with Van Heflin, who did a commendable job as Curly, the marshal) proved more than equal to the dramatic challenge of *Stagecoach* and added a new dimension to his role. While people like Slim Pickens, Red Buttons, Bob Cummings, and Stefanie Powers contributed to the aesthetic massacre, Bing received attention for his witty, thoroughly convincing performance. He was aware that Thomas Mitchell had won an Oscar in 1939 as the "sodden surgeon" who, with the town prostitute, is expelled from Dryfork. Unwilling to imitate Mitchell, he develops his own character and stakes an equal claim on the part.

Perhaps it was not a brilliant good-bye, but Bing's Doc Boone was a solid enough exit from the screen. When Bing won his Academy Award, he said, "All I can say is that it sure is a wonderful world when a tired old crooner like me can walk away with this hunk of crockery." Whether through modesty or lack of confidence, Bing consistently refused to think of himself as an actor of substance and worth. The handful of serious performances prove him wrong. It is these, not his sequined musicals, that provide the truest glitter of his career.

10:10 P.M.—Sunday,
December 19, 1976

BROADWAY FAREWELL

The stage at New York's Uris Theatre was dark and bare, with the exception of a lone spotlight and a single stool. It was the final night of *Bing on Broadway*, and the audience was hushed. Bing was about to sing his last song. It had been forty-five years since he had appeared on a New York stage. He was seventy-five. Everyone seemed to feel that it was more than the finale of one show or the end of one Broadway run.

Since seven-thirty that evening, when the curtain rose, it had been a joyful reunion. Mr. Casual had talked to the audience as if he were sitting around his living room with a couple of old friends. He had told anecdotes about his career, those famous pockets in his cheeks ballooning as he pronounced his beloved ten-dollar words. He had harmonized with his old friend, Rosemary Clooney, and scat-sung with the Joe Bushkin Quartet.

He had made fun of Bob Hope ("He's had so many face lifts, he blows his nose on his ski-slope knees"). And he had made fun of himself ("At my age, I'm just happy to have a pulse." . . . "My career has spanned leading ladies from Mary Pickford to Liza Minnelli"). He had told about a recent cab ride: "You know, you look a lot like Bing Crosby," the cabbie had said. "Oh, no," Bing protested. "I'm much better looking than Bing Crosby." The cab driver looked back in his mirror and seemed to accept the assessment. The two had driven on silently for a while. Then, unable to let the situation lie, the cabbie had shrugged, "Well, you wouldn't mind looking like Bing Crosby if you had his money."

He had even danced a little to the nostalgic sound of the Billy Byers Orchestra. Mostly, however, Bing had sung. He had "reached back into the fire and pulled out a few chestnuts," among them "Sweet Leilani," "Pennies from Heaven," "I Surrender, Dear," "South of the Border," "Swinging on a Star," "Blue Skies," "Don't Fence Me In," and—appropriate to both the star and the season—"White Christmas."

The show had opened with "Where the Blue of the Night." What would be Bing Crosby's farewell? Suddenly, he walked out from the wings. For all of the unchanged voice and charm he had exhibited until now, he seemed a little frail, his blue eyes a little sad. "Everyone seems to have a song that sums up his career," he said as he seated himself on the stool. "Frank's got 'My Way.' Tony's got 'This Is All I

Ask.' Well, now I've got one too."

The song, "That's What Life Is All About," was his final moment on that final evening. It brought the house down. Some people were crying. Others jumped to their feet and yelled, "Bravo! Bravo!" He stood before his audience, bowed low, and walked offstage. They brought him back again and again.

As the lights went up and the curtain started to descend, Bing looked out at his fans. "I love you," he said.

BIBLIOGRAPHY

Buxton, Frank. *The Big Broadcast, 1920-1950*. Viking Press, New York, 1972.

Capra, Frank. *Frank Capra: The Name Above the Title*. The Macmillan Company, New York, 1971.

Crosby, Bing. *Call Me Lucky*. Simon & Schuster, New York, 1953.

Crosby, Kathryn. *Bing and Other Things*. Meredith Press, New York, 1967.

Crosby, Ted. *The Story of Bing Crosby*. The World Publishing Company, Cleveland, Ohio, 1946.

Green, Stanley. *Ring Bells! Sing Songs!: Broadway Musicals of the 1930's*. Galahad Books, New York, 1971.

Michael, Paul (ed.). *Movie Greats; The Players, Directors, Producers*. Garland Books, New York, 1969.

Michael, Paul (ed.). *The American Movies; The History, Films, Awards*. Garland Books, New York, 1969.

Thompson, Charles. *Bing; An Authorized Biography*. David McKay Company, Inc., New York, 1975.

Springer, John. *All Talking! All Singing! All Dancing!*. Citadel Press, New York, 1966.

THE FILMS OF BING CROSBY

The director's name follows the release date. A (c) following the release date indicates that the film is in color. Sp. indicates screenplay and b/o indicates based on.

Feature Films

1. KING OF JAZZ. Universal, 1930 (c). *John Murray Anderson.* Cast: Paul Whiteman, John Boles, Laura La Plante, George Gershwin, the Brox Sisters, the Rhythm Boys with Bing Crosby.

2. THE BIG BROADCAST. Paramount, 1932. *Frank Tuttle.* Sp: George Marion, Jr., b/o play *Wild Waves* by William Ford Manley. Cast: Stuart Erwin, Leila Hyams, Sharon Lynne, George Burns and Gracie Allen, Kate Smith, the Mills Brothers, the Boswell Sisters, Vincent Lopez and his orchestra, Cab Calloway and his band, Arthur Tracy.

3. COLLEGE HUMOR. Paramount, 1933. *Wesley Ruggles.* Sp: Claude Binyon and Frank Butler, b/o story by Dean Fales. Cast: Jack Oakie, Richard Arlen, Mary Carlisle, George Burns and Gracie Allen.

4. TOO MUCH HARMONY. Paramount, 1933. *Edward Sutherland.* Sp: Harry Ruskin, b/o story by Joseph L. Mankiewicz. Cast: Jack Oakie, Skeets Gallagher, Judith Allen, Harry Green, Lilyan Tashman, Ned Sparks, Kitty Kelly.

5. GOING HOLLYWOOD. MGM, 1933. *Raoul Walsh.* Sp: Donald Ogden Stewart, b/o story by Frances Marion. Cast: Marion Davies, Fifi D'Orsay, Stuart Erwin, Ned Sparks, Patsy Kelly.

6. WE'RE NOT DRESSING. Paramount, 1934. *Norman Taurog.* Sp: Horace Jackson, Francis Martin, and George Marion, Jr., b/o story by Benjamin Glazer. Cast: Carole Lombard, George Burns and Gracie Allen, Ethel Merman, Leon Errol, Raymond (Ray) Milland.

7. SHE LOVES ME NOT. Paramount, 1934. *Elliott Nugent.* Sp: Benjamin Glazer, b/o novel by Edward Hope and play by Howard Lindsay. Cast: Miriam Hopkins, Kitty Carlisle, Edward Nugent, Henry Stephenson, Lynne Overman. Remade in 1955 as *How to be Very, Very Popular.*

8. HERE IS MY HEART. Paramount, 1934. *Frank Tuttle.* Sp: Edwin Justus Mayer and Harlan Thompson, b/o play *The Grand Duchess and the Waiter* by Alfred Savoir. Cast: Kitty Carlisle, Roland Young, Alison Skipworth, Reginald Owen, William Frawley. Previously filmed in 1926.

147

9. MISSISSIPPI. Paramount, 1935. *Edward A. Sutherland*. Sp: Francis Martin and Jack Cunningham, adap. by Herbert Fields and Claude Binyon, b/o novel *Magnolia* by Booth Tarkington. Cast: W. C. Fields, Joan Bennett, Queenie Smith, Claude Gillingwater, John Miljan.

10. TWO FOR TONIGHT. Paramount, 1935. *Frank Tuttle*. Sp: George Marion, Jr. and Jane Storm with additional dialogue by Harry Ruskin, b/o play by Max Lief and J. O. Lief. Cast: Joan Bennett, Mary Boland, Lynne Overman, Thelma Todd, Douglas Fowley.

11. THE BIG BROADCAST OF 1936. Paramount, 1935. *Norman Taurog*. Sp: Walter DeLeon, Francis Martin and Ralph Spence. Cast: Jack Oakie, George Burns and Gracie Allen, Lyda Roberti, Ethel Merman, Amos 'n' Andy.

12. ANYTHING GOES (TOPS IS THE LIMIT). Paramount, 1936. *Lewis Milestone*. B/o play by Howard Lindsay and Russel Crouse. Cast: Ethel Merman, Charles Ruggles, Ida Lupino, Arthur Treacher. Remade in 1956.

13. RHYTHM ON THE RANGE. Paramount, 1936. *Norman Taurog*. Sp: Walter DeLeon, Francis Martin, John C. Moffitt and Sidney Salkow, b/o story by Mervin J. Houser. Cast: Frances Farmer, Bob Burns, Martha Raye, Samuel S. Hinds, Warren Hymer. Remade as *Pardners* (1956).

14. PENNIES FROM HEAVEN. Columbia, 1936. *Norman Z. McLeod*. Sp: Jo Swerling, b/o *The Peacock's Feather* by Katharine Leslie Moore. Cast: Madge Evans, Edith Fellows, Donald Meek, Louis Armstrong.

15. WAIKIKI WEDDING. Paramount, 1937. *Frank Tuttle*. Sp: Frank Butler, Don Hartman, Walter DeLeon and Francis Martin, b/o story by Frank Butler and Don Hartman. Cast: Bob Burns, Martha Raye, Shirley Ross, Leif Erickson, Anthony Quinn.

16. DOUBLE OR NOTHING. Paramount, 1937. *Theodore Reed*. Sp: Charles Lederer, Erwin Gelsey, John C. Moffitt, and Duke Atterberry, b/o story by M. Coates Webster. Cast: Martha Raye, Andy Devine, William Frawley, Mary Carlisle.

17. DOCTOR RHYTHM. Paramount, 1938. *Frank Tuttle*. Adap. by Jo Swerling and Richard Connell, b/o "The Badge of Policeman O'Roon" by O. Henry. Cast: Mary Carlisle, Beatrice Lillie, Andy Devine, Sterling Holloway, Louis Armstrong.

18. SING YOU SINNERS. Paramount, 1938. *Wesley Ruggles*. Sp: Claude Binyon, b/o his story. Cast: Fred MacMurray, Ellen Drew, Donald O'Connor, Elizabeth Patterson.

19. PARIS HONEYMOON. Paramount, 1939. *Frank Tuttle*. Sp: Frank Butler

and Don Hartman, b/o story by Angela Sherwood. Cast: Franciska Gaal, Akim Tamiroff, Shirley Ross, Edward Everett Horton, Ben Blue.

20. EAST SIDE OF HEAVEN. Universal, 1939. *David Butler*. Sp: William Conselman, b/o story by David Butler and Herbert Polesie. Cast: Joan Blondell, Mischa Auer, Irene Hervey, C. Aubrey Smith, Baby Sandy.

21. THE STAR MAKER. Paramount, 1939. *Roy Del Ruth*. Sp: Frank Butler, Don Hartman, and Arthur Caesar, b/o story by Arthur Caesar and William A. Pierce, suggested by the career of Gus Edwards. Cast: Louise Campbell, Linda Ware, Ned Sparks, Thurston Hall.

22. ROAD TO SINGAPORE. Paramount, 1940. *Victor Schertzinger*. Sp: Don Hartman and Frank Butler, b/o story by Harry Hervey. Cast: Dorothy Lamour, Bob Hope, Charles Coburn, Anthony Quinn, Jerry Colonna.

23. IF I HAD MY WAY. Universal, 1940. *David Butler*. Sp: William Conselman and James V. Kern. Cast: Gloria Jean, Charles Winninger, El Brendel, Allyn Joslyn, Blanche Ring, Eddie Leonard, Grace LaRue.

24. RHYTHM ON THE RIVER. Paramount, 1940. *Victor Schertzinger*. Sp: Dwight Taylor, b/o story by Billy Wilder and Jacques Thery. Cast: Mary Martin, Basil Rathbone, Oscar Levant, John Scott Trotter, Wingy Mannone.

25. ROAD TO ZANZIBAR. Paramount, 1941. *Victor Schertzinger*. Sp: Frank Butler and Don Hartman, b/o story by Don Hartman and Sy Bartlett. Cast: Dorothy Lamour, Bob Hope, Una Merkel, Eric Blore, Joan Marsh.

26. BIRTH OF THE BLUES. Paramount, 1941. *Victor Schertzinger*. Sp: Harry Tugend and Walter DeLeon, b/o story by Harry Tugend. Cast: Mary Martin, Brian Donlevy, Eddie Anderson, Jack Teagarden, J. Carrol Naish, Ruby Elzy, Harry Barris, Perry Botkin.

27. HOLIDAY INN. Paramount, 1942. *Mark Sandrich*. Sp: Claude Binyon, adap. by Elmer Rice, b/o original idea by Irving Berlin. Cast: Fred Astaire, Marjorie Reynolds, Virginia Dale, Walter Abel.

28. ROAD TO MOROCCO. Paramount, 1942. *David Butler*. Sp: Frank Butler and Don Hartman. Cast: Bob Hope, Dorothy Lamour, Anthony Quinn, Dona Drake.

29. STAR SPANGLED RHYTHM. Paramount, 1942. *George Marshall*. Sp: Harry Tugend. Cast: Victor Moore, Betty Hutton, Eddie Bracken, Walter Abel, Bob Hope, Fred MacMurray, Franchot Tone, Dorothy Lamour, Veronica Lake, Alan Ladd.

30. DIXIE. Paramount, 1943 (c). *A. Edward Sutherland*. Sp: Karl Tunberg and

Darrell Ware, adap. by Claude Binyon, b/o story by William Rankin. Cast: Dorothy Lamour, Marjorie Reynolds, Billy De Wolfe, Lynne Overman, Eddie Foy, Jr.

31. GOING MY WAY. Paramount, 1944. *Leo McCarey*. Sp: Frank Butler and Frank Cavett, b/o story by Leo McCarey. Cast: Risë Stevens, Barry Fitzgerald, Jean Heather, Frank McHugh, Gene Lockhart.

32. HERE COME THE WAVES. Paramount, 1945. *Mark Sandrich*. Sp: Allan Scott, Ken Englund and Zion Myers. Cast: Betty Hutton, Sonny Tufts, Ann Doran, Gwen Crawford.

33. DUFFY'S TAVERN. Paramount, 1945. *Hal Walker*. Sp: Melvin Frank and Norman Panama, with additional sketches by Abram S. Burrows, Barney Dean, George White, Eddie Davis and Matt Brooks. Cast: Ed Gardner, Victor Moore, Marjorie Reynolds, Barry Sullivan, Eddie Green, Betty Hutton, Paulette Goddard, Alan Ladd, Dorothy Lamour, Eddie Bracken, Brian Donlevy, Sonny Tufts, Gary, Phillip, Dennis and Lin Crosby.

34. ROAD TO UTOPIA. Paramount, 1946. *Hal Walker*. Sp: Norman Panama and Melvin Frank. Cast: Bob Hope, Dorothy Lamour, Robert Benchley, Douglass Dumbrille, Hillary Brooke.

35. THE BELLS OF ST. MARY'S. RKO, 1945. *Leo McCarey*. Sp: Dudley Nichols. Cast: Ingrid Bergman, Henry Travers, Joan Carroll, Martha Sleeper.

36. BLUE SKIES. Paramount, 1946 (c). *Stuart Heisler*. Sp: Arthur Sheekman, adap. by Allan Scott, b/o an original idea by Irving Berlin. Cast: Fred Astaire, Joan Caulfield, Billy De Wolfe, Olga San Juan.

37. VARIETY GIRL. Paramount, 1947. *George Marshall*. Sp: Edmund Hartmann, Frank Tashlin, Robert Welch and Monte Brice. Cast: Mary Hatcher, Olga San Juan, De Forest Kelley, William Demarest, Frank Faylen, Bob Hope, Pearl Bailey, Dorothy Lamour.

38. WELCOME STRANGER. Paramount, 1947. *Elliott Nugent*. Sp: Arthur Sheekman, adap. by Arthur Sheekman and N. Richard Nash, b/o story by Frank Butler. Cast: Joan Caulfield, Barry Fitzgerald, Frank Faylen, Elizabeth Patterson.

39. ROAD TO RIO. Paramount, 1948. *Norman Z. McLeod*. Sp: Edmund Beloin and Jack Rose, b/o their story. Cast: Bob Hope, Dorothy Lamour, Gale Sondergaard, Frank Faylen, Jerry Colonna, the Wiere Brothers, the Andrews Sisters.

40. THE EMPEROR WALTZ. Paramount, 1948 (c). *Billy Wilder*. Sp: Charles Brackett and Billy Wilder. Cast: Joan Fontaine, Richard Haydn, Sig Ruman, Lucile Watson, Roland Culver.

41. A CONNECTICUT YANKEE IN KING ARTHUR'S COURT. Paramount, 1949 (c). *Tay Garnett*. Sp: Edmund Beloin, b/o novel by Mark Twain. Cast: William Bendix, Sir Cedric Hardwicke, Rhonda Fleming, Henry Wilcoxon. Previously filmed in 1921 and 1931.

42. TOP O' THE MORNING. Paramount, 1949 (c). *David Miller*. Sp: Edmund Beloin and Richard Breen. Cast: Ann Blyth, Barry Fitzgerald, Hume Cronyn, Eileen Crowe.

43. RIDING HIGH. Paramount, 1950. *Frank Capra*. Sp: Robert Riskin with additional dialogue by Melville Shavelson and Jack Rose, b/o story by Mark Hellinger. Cast: Coleen Gray, Charles Bickford, Frances Gifford, William Demarest, Clarence Muse, Ward Bond, Raymond Walburn, Oliver Hardy. A remake of *Broadway Bill* (1934).

44. MR. MUSIC. Paramount, 1950. *Richard Haydn*. Sp: Arthur Sheekman, suggested by play *Accent on Youth* by Samson Raphaelson. Cast: Nancy Olson, Charles Coburn, Ruth Hussey, Robert Stack, Tom Ewell, Marge and Gower Champion, Groucho Marx, Dorothy Kirsten, Peggy Lee.

45. HERE COMES THE GROOM. Paramount, 1951. *Frank Capra*. Sp: Virginia Van Upp, Liam O'Brien, and Myles Connelly, b/o story by Robert Riskin and Liam O'Brien. Cast: Jane Wyman, Franchot Tone, Alexis Smith, Jacky Gencel, Beverly Washburn, Anna Maria Alberghetti, Dorothy Lamour, Phil Harris, Louis Armstrong.

46. JUST FOR YOU. Paramount, 1952 (c). *Elliott Nugent*. Sp: Robert Carson, b/o *Famous* by Stephen Vincent Benet. Cast: Jane Wyman, Ethel Barrymore, Natalie Wood, Robert Arthur, Cora Witherspoon.

47. ROAD TO BALI. Paramount, 1952 (c). *Hal Walker*. Sp: Frank Butler, Hal Kanter and William Morrow, b/o story by Frank Butler and Harry Tugend. Cast: Bob Hope, Dorothy Lamour, Murvyn Vye, Peter Coe.

48. LITTLE BOY LOST. Paramount, 1953. *George Seaton*. Sp: George Seaton, b/o story by Marghanita Laski. Cast: Claude Dauphin, Christian Fourçade, Gabrielle Dorziat, Nicole Maurey.

49. WHITE CHRISTMAS. Paramount, 1954 (c). *Michael Curtiz*. Sp: Norman Panama, Melvin Frank and Norman Krasna. Cast: Danny Kaye, Rosemary Clooney, Vera-Ellen, Dean Jagger, Mary Wickes.

50. THE COUNTRY GIRL. Paramount, 1954. *George Seaton*. Sp: George Seaton, b/o play by Clifford Odets. Cast: Grace Kelly, William Holden, Anthony Ross, Gene Reynolds.

51. ANYTHING GOES. Paramount, 1956 (c). *Robert Lewis*. Sp: Sidney

Sheldon, b/o play by Guy Bolton and P. G. Wodehouse, revised by Howard Lindsay and Russel Crouse. Cast: Donald O'Connor, Jeanmaire, Mitzi Gaynor, Phil Harris. Previously filmed in 1936.

52. HIGH SOCIETY. MGM, 1956 (c). *Charles Walters*. Sp: John Patrick, b/o play *The Philadelphia Story* by Philip Barry. Cast: Grace Kelly, Frank Sinatra, Celeste Holm, John Lund. A musical remake of *The Philadelphia Story* (1940).

53. MAN ON FIRE. MGM, 1957. *Ranald MacDougall*. Sp: Ranald MacDougall, b/o story by Malvin Wald and Jack Jacobs. Cast: Inger Stevens, Mary Fickett, E. G. Marshall, Malcolm Brodrick, Richard Eastham.

54. SAY ONE FOR ME. 20th Century-Fox, 1959 (c). *Frank Tashlin*. Sp: Robert O'Brien. Cast: Debbie Reynolds, Robert Wagner, Ray Walston, Frank McHugh.

55. HIGH TIME. 20th Century-Fox, 1960 (c). *Blake Edwards*. Sp: Tom and Frank Waldman, b/o story by Garson Kanin. Cast: Fabian, Tuesday Weld, Nicole Maurey, Richard Beymer.

56. THE ROAD TO HONG KONG. United Artists, 1962 (c). *Norman Panama*. Sp: Norman Panama and Melvin Frank. Cast: Bob Hope, Joan Collins, Dorothy Lamour, Robert Morley, Peter Sellers.

57. ROBIN AND THE 7 HOODS. Warner Brothers, 1964 (c). *Gordon Douglas*. Sp: David R. Schwartz. Cast: Frank Sinatra, Dean Martin, Peter Falk, Barbara Rush, Sammy Davis, Jr., Victor Buono, Edward G. Robinson.

58. STAGECOACH. 20th Century-Fox, 1966 (c). *Gordon Douglas*. Sp: Joseph Landon, b/o screenplay by Dudley Nichols from a story by Ernest Haycox. Cast: Ann-Margret, Michael Connors, Van Heflin, Red Buttons, Bob Cummings, Slim Pickens, Keenan Wynn. A remake of the 1939 film.

ADDITIONAL MOVIES WITH BING CROSBY

Unbilled Guest Appearances with the Rhythm Boys

1. REACHING FOR THE MOON, 1930.
2. CONFESSIONS OF A CO-ED, 1931.

Mack Sennett Shorts (Released 1931-1933)

1. JUST ONE MORE CHANCE.
2. BILLBOARD GIRL.
3. I SURRENDER, DEAR.
4. SING, SING, SING.
5. DREAM HOUSE.
6. THE BLUE OF THE NIGHT.

Cameos

1. MY FAVORITE BLONDE. Paramount, 1942.
2. THE PRINCESS AND THE PIRATE. RKO, 1944.
3. MY FAVORITE BRUNETTE. Paramount, 1947.
4. THE GREATEST SHOW ON EARTH. Paramount, 1952.
5. SON OF PALEFACE. Paramount, 1952.
6. SCARED STIFF. Paramount, 1952.
7. ALIAS JESSE JAMES. United Artists, 1959.
8. PEPE. Columbia, 1960.
9. LET'S MAKE LOVE. 20th Century-Fox, 1960.

Voice Only

1. CHECK AND DOUBLE CHECK, 1930. (with the Rhythm Boys)
2. OUT OF THIS WORLD. Paramount, 1945.
3. THE ADVENTURES OF ICHABOD AND MR. TOAD. RKO, 1949.
4. CINERAMA'S RUSSIAN ADVENTURE. Cinerama, 1966.

Anthologies

1. THE ROAD TO HOLLYWOOD, 1943.
2. THE SOUND OF LAUGHTER, 1963.

INDEX

156

ABOUT THE AUTHOR

Barbara Bauer is a free-lance writer based in New York. Educated at Columbia and a former executive with a Broadway producing house, she often writes on film and theater subjects. In addition to women's magazines, her work has appeared in *The Los Angeles Times, Bijou, Film Information* and *Change Magazine for Higher Learning.* She is the author of *Judge Horton and the Scottsboro Boys* (Ballantine), an adaptation of the television movie.

ABOUT THE EDITOR

Ted Sennett is the author of *Warner Brothers Presents*, a tribute to the great Warners films of the thirties and forties, and of *Lunatics and Lovers*, on the long-vanished but well-remembered "screwball" movie comedies of the past. He is the editor of *The Movie Buff's Book, The Old-Time Radio Book*, and *The Movie Buff's Book: Two.* He is also the editor of *Bijou: The Magazine of the Movies.*